Glimpses of MARATHA SOCIO-ECONOMIC HISTORY

K.N. CHITNIS

ATLANTIC

PUBLISHERS & DISTRIBUTORS (P) LTD

Published by

ATLANTIC

PUBLISHERS & DISTRIBUTORS (P) LTD

7/22, Ansari Road, Darya Ganj, New Delhi-110002
Phones : +91-11-40775252, 23273880, 23275880, 23280451
Fax : +91-11-23285873
Web : www.atlanticbooks.com
E-mail : orders@atlanticbooks.com
Branch Office
5, Nallathambi Street, Wallajah Road, Chennai-600002
Phones : +91-44-64611085
E-mail : chennai@atlanticbooks.com

Printed in India at Nice Printing Press, A-33/3A, Site-IV, Industrial Area, Sahibabad, Ghaziabad, U.P.

Preface

The present book has developed out of the special lectures which I delivered at the instance of the Shivaji University, Kolhapur, on the Southern Maratha Country (A.D. 1650-1818): An Administrative and Economic Study. When I thought of bringing out these lectures in print I added some more material to them on various small topics covered by the title. Finally to make it more comprehensive, a small chapter on the Social Life in this area has also been added. Care has been taken to see that the whole narration is a coherent and well-connected account.

The book gives a good idea of the Maratha administration, and also of the economic and social life of the people in this important area, which was indirectly governed by the Peshwas in the beginning, and which was under direct Peshwa rule during the later period.

The book presents a micro-study of this area based on original, unpublished archival material. Hence at times the narration is full of facts and figures, and this gives the authenticity and the validity to the whole treatment. I have tried my best to present the highly technical matter in an intelligible manner. There is some variation in the manner in which the revenue figures are expressed, about which a separate note is given. Readers are advised to consult this note for understanding the meaning of these figures properly. This has been necessitated, because the difficult Peshwa method of writing revenue figures has been given in a way that is understandable to the readers who are not acquainted with that system.

The book contains an account of the administration, economy and the social structure prevailing in the Southern Maratha Country under the Marathas. As the Marathas were ruling there, the administrative system and the economy of the country were highly influenced by them, containing as they did a number of Maratha elements. The social structure, customs and manners were also affected, though to a lesser, extent. All the features of this pattern came to exist in this area, though with minor modifications, almost down to the middle of the 19th century, when by coming in contact with the British ideas and institutions, the whole society rapidly underwant changes in a big way. Hence references to some sources beyond the Peshwa period, but before the middle of the 19th century, are occasionally found. Again for obvious reasons, a compact title like "Glimpses of Maratha Socio-Economic History" is given, although the book contains an account of the administration of that area as well. Unless one has a good idea of the administrative system prevailing then, one cannot properly grasp the intricacies of the revenue system as it includes various types of inam lands, alienated revenue and the like.

Again as this Maratha socio-economic account is only about a small area known as Southern Maratha Country or roughly the Krishna-Tungabhadra Doab in North Karnataka, it gives us only glimpses of social and economic systems of the Marathas, and not the complete picture. Hence the title has been kept as *Glimpses of Maratha Socio-Economic History*.

Much has been written on the political history of the Marathas, covering their activities both in North and South India. Of late, the trend has been to write the social and economic history of the Marathas. A few monographs and stray articles have appeared on such topics as trade and commerce, social life, coinage and feudalism during the Maratha period. However, unless an intensive study of such aspects based on the original primary sources, available not only in Modi but also in the various regional languages in the areas where the Marathas once ruled, is made, the study of the life of people under the Marathas will not be complete.

An attempt is made in this treatise to analyse the political, social and economic life of the people in a tract which was not only under Maratha rule for over a century, but which also served as the Southern Gateway of the Marathas underlining its strategical importance. As this region, the region of the Krishna-Tungabhadra Doab, had an admixture of Vijayanagara, Adilshahi, Maratha and indigenous systems of administration, and economic features, its study for understanding the Maratha administration and the life of the people under Maratha rule in this region becomes highly interesting and instructive. In fact, the Maratha administration in different regions outside Maharashtra presents a Complex phenomenon that was affected by the historical antecedents of those respective areas. Hence one finds many minor variations in the administrative patterns of the Marathas in different regions such as Gujarat, Malwa, Orissa and Karnatak.

There have been some works written on this region earlier. In 1869 E.W. West wrote a Memoir of the States of the Southern Maratha

Country, and later B.P. Modak dealt with this region in his Marathi book entitled *Kolhapur Va Karnatak Prantatil Rajye Va Samsthane Yancha Itihas: Uttarardha, Bhag 2: Karanataka Prantatil Samsthanancha Itihas*, in 1880. Both the above works mostly deal with the political history of the region, although Modak gives some information about economic matters taken from the gazetteers. Finally R.D. Choksey has written a book in 1963 on the economic life in the Bombay Karnatak during the period 1818-1839. None of these works deals comprehensively with the administrative, social and economic aspects of the history of this region under the Marathas, and that is precisely the subject matter of the present treatise. And this is based, as pointed out in the section on "Sources" in Chapter I, on a large number of original unpublished sources, not tapped by any other historian so far. Most of this source material is taken from the Pune, Bombay, Kolhapr and Karnatak Archives, as well as from the Bharat Itihas Samshodhak Mandal Archives. I am thankful to the authorities of all these Archives for kindly permitting me to utilise their source material for research. My thanks are due to the Jayakar Library, University of Poona, Pune, the Gokhale Institute Library, Pune, the Bharat Itihas Samshodhak Mandal Library, Pune, the Mythic Society Library, Bangalore, and other libraries where I consulted the relevant books for my research work while writing the present treatise.

I thank my wife Radha for her constant encouragement to me in all my academic endeavours. My sons, Prafulla and Shashank, have prepared on the computer the chart on the "Castes in the Southern Maratha Country". I give them my good wishes. Finally, I record my gratefulness to the Atlantic Publishers, and to their Managing Director, Dr. K.R. Gupta, for publishing this book with great care.

Pune, K.N. CHITNIS

17-12-1992

Contents

Abbreviations

BISMA	:	Bharat Itihas Samshodhak Mandal Archives
Dilerjangi	:	Kitab Nawab Mustatabamo Allah Alakab Nawab Dalerkhan Bahadur Dalerjang Yanche Khandancha Ahawal
HS	:	*House of Shivaji*
KJ	:	Karnatak Jamav, Pune Archives.
LD	:	Lakshmeshwar Desai Daftar, Bharat Itihas Samshodhak Mandal, Pune
PA	:	Pune Archives
Sannika	:	*Samshodhanasathi Nivadalele Kagad* (Documents Selected for research, in Pune Archives)
SCS	:	*Shiva-Charitra-Sahitya*
SSRPD	:	*Selections from Satara Raja's and Peshwas' Diaries*
TKK	:	*Tarabai-Kalina Kagadapatre*

List of Maps and Chart, Etc.

Note on Land Measure Figures and Revenue Figures

Both the quantity of lands and the amount of money are expressed here in this book in three different ways. They are given either under four heads or three heads or two heads. When expressed under four heads (for example, 73-2-1-1), the first shows complete units, the second one-fourth of the first, the third one-forth of the second and the fourth one-fourth of the third. Under the second, third and fourth heads, the figure is never 4 or more than 4, the maximum here would be only 3, for when it is four quarters it automatically becomes one under the next higher head. Thus in the above example, if the figure under the fourth head becomes 4, then it is shifted to the third head which now becomes 2 instead of remaining 1, and the fourth head becomes 0. If the above expression is in terms of *mars* of lands, it would mean that the first head stands for one *mar* (36 bighas), the second for one-fourth of this (9 bighas), the third for one-foruth of the second (2.25 bighas or 450 pands) and the fourth for one-fourth of the third (0.5625 bighas or 112.50 pands). In respect of *hons*, it would mean that the first head stands for one complete *hon*, the second for one-fourth of this (one *dharana*), the third for one-fourth of the second (one *duval*), and the fourth for one-fourth of the third (one *visa*). So an expression like 23-3-1-2 *hons* would mean 23 *hons*, 3 *dharanas*, 1 *duval* and 2 *visas*. This method was generally followed during the Shivaji and Peshwa periods. However, during the Company period the *hons* began to be converted into rupees when the practice of expressing the amounts slightly changed. Instead of four heads, only three heads came to be used, the first standing for the complete unit of the rupee, the second for its 16th part and the third for its 64th part. In other words, the first stood for the complete *rupee*, the second for the *anna*, and the third for the *paisa*. In this method the second and the third heads of the Maratha method are expressed in one head only, that is, in the second head. Thus, to take the above example 23-3-1-2 *hons* could also be expressed as 23-13-2 *hons*, in which case it would mean 23 *hons*, 13 *duvals* and 2 *visas*. Here 3 *dharanas* are included in 13 *duvals*. If the expression 23-3-1-2 is in respect of rupees, then it would mean 23 rupees, 3 *pavalis* (four-anna pieces), I anna and 2 paise. If expressed under three heads, it would be Rs. 23-13-2 which means 23 rupees, 13 annas and 2 paise. Here 3 *pavalis* are included in 13 annas. Generally the latter method was followed during the Company period, although the Maratha method was not completely done away with. In some cases the decimal method also is used in this book which shows how the Peshwa method could be expressed in modern ways.

I

Introduction

The Southern Maratha Country was enclosed by the river Krishna in the North and the river Tungabhadra in the South. The Krishna-Tungabhadra Doab forms a separate geographical unit physically. At one time politically also it had formed a separate unit, though not always. Under the Peshwas it was known as the Karnatak Doab and also as Prant Karnatak.

Connotation of the term

After the defeat of the Marathas in 1818, the British constituted this area into a separate political and administrative unit with some minor changes, and wanted to include it in the Madras Presidency. But after much discussion among the British Officers, it was finally incorporated into the Bombay Presidency, giving it a separate name "Southern Maratha Country" "The District known politically as the Southern Maratha Country", says Edward West, "corresponds nearly with the Maratha geographical division of the 'Carnatic', or country situated between the rivers Krishna and Tongbuddra—a tract frequently referred to during the Maratha campaigns of the early part of the 19th century as the 'Doab'"[1]

This is, however, a loose definition, as West himself has admitted. Originally Sir Thomas Munro first coined this term, but was loosely adopted for this area. The core of the Southern Maratha Country was the Krishna-Tungabhadra Doab, but because of the peculiar historical antecedents some other territories came to be loosely associated with this tract. Under the British it comprised the collectorates of Belgaum Dharwad and Kaladgi (*i.e.*, the portion of the later Bijapur district to the

1. Edward West, in *A Memoir of the states of the Southern Maratha Country* (Bombay, 1869), introduction, p. v.

south of the Krishna) and the princely states of Savanur, Kittur, Nargund, Ramdurg, Mudhol, Jamkhandi, Shedbal (Kagwad), Nippani and Chinchni. Some of the areas in this tract were held by the princely states lying outside this tract. Such states were Miraj, Sangli, Kurundwad and Tasgaon. As these states had some of their territories even to the north of the Krishna and Kolhapur, sometimes they were also vaguely associated with this term. This area called Southern Maratha Country was first of all administered and politically superintended by the Principal Collector at Dharwad till 1836 when the collector of Belgaum was made the Political Agent who was also politically superintending Kolhapur. After 1843 Kolhapur was separated from him. After some years the Political Agent of Kolhapur himself began to discharge, in addition, the political duties of the Southern Maratha Country.

Following the Maratha tradition and the geographical features of the region, only the land lying between the river Krishna in the north and the Tungabhadra in the South has been included here in the term Southern Maratha Country. But when the term Prant Karnatak is used, some areas beyond these rivers, namely, Taluka Athani in the North and rarely Taluka Harihar in the South are also included. Hence for the purpose of this study, the term Southern Maratha Country includes both the above terms, namely, the Krishna-Tungabhadra Doab, which is a geographical term, and Prant Karnatak, which was a political term.

Geographical Features

History is said to be geography set in motion. The geographical features of the region have, among other things, tremendously influenced the social, political and economic life of that area. Hence a study of the geographical configuration in understanding the history of a country can hardly be exaggerated.

This Southern Maratha Country forms an independent geographical unit. It includes the present districts of Belgaum and Dharwad wholly and the district of Bijapur south of the Krishna. Geographically it can be divided into three natural divisions, namely, the *Malenadu*, the *Gadinadu* and the *Belavalanadu* The Malenadu is a hilly area getting the highest rainfall in the whole Doab It includes a small strip of territory, namely parts of Belgaum and Khanapur Talukas (in Belgaum district), the whole of Kalghatgi and Hangal, and parts of Dharwad, Hubli Kundgol Shiggaon. Haveri, Byadgi and Hirekerur talukas (in Dharwad district). The Gadinadu, lying to the north-east of the Malenadu, includes Chikkodi, Hukkeri, Gokak, Belgaum, Bailhongal, and Khanpur talukas wholly or partly (in Belgaum district), Navalgund, Dharwad, Hubli, Kundgol, Savanur, Haveri, Byadgi, Hirekerur and Ranebennur talukas wholly or partly (in Dharwad district).

The Belavalanadu includes Athani, Raibag, Gokak, Ramdurg and Saudatti talukas wholly or partly (in Belgaum district), Nargund, Navalgund, Shirhatti, Ron, Gadag and Mundargi talukas wholly or partly (in Dharwad district), and all the tract of Bijapur district south of the Krishna. Almost the whole of the Belgaum district is a hilly tract, especially the Malenad and Gadinad strips having a number of small ranges of hills. The Dharwad district has comparatively fewer hills. In Dharwad, Hubli, Nargund, Ron, Mundargi and Ranebennur areas one finds some solitary hills. In the Kaladgi area we have again a number of small hills.

The Doab receives both the south-western and northeastern rains. The Malenad gets the highest rainfall, from 50" to 100", the Gadinad from 25" to 50" and the Belavalanad from 15" to 25". Besides rains, the region is fed by two big rivers the Krishna in the north and the Tungabhadra in the south and by a network of their tributaries and other rivulets and streams. The *Ghataprabha* and *Malaprabha* are two important tributaries of the *Krishna*, the *Agami* in the Athani taluka, the *Dudhganga* in the Chikodi taluka being some streams. In the Dharwad district the *Varada* and *Kumudvati* are the important tributaries of the Tungabhadra, the Hirehalla, Bennihalla. Tuparihalla, Bendatihalla being small streams. The *Shalmala* and *Dharma* are the two rivulets. All the streams flow in the northern part of the district, the Shalmala and the Dharma flow in the Western part.

The principal crops grown in this area were jawar, wheat, sugarcane, rice, cotton, chillies, groundnuts and tobacco. Rice was grown in the Malenad, sugarcane mostly in the Gadinad, jawar both in the Gadinad and Belavalanad, cotton and wheat mostly in Belavalanad. Tobacco was grown only in the Nippani region which was in the Gadinad. Roughly one can say that in Belgaum district rice grew in Malenad, sugarcane in Gadinad, wheat in Belavalanad, tobacco in the Nippani region, and the rest both in Gadinad and Belavalanad.

SOURCES

The present monograph is almost entirely based on unpublished original archival sources, although it has received corroborations from published sources. Only some parts from the introduction relating to the political developments in this region are written with the help of the published original source material, which also are corroborated by other works of a later date. The nature and type of the subject itself are such that they are to be based on unpublished material, for no work of this type on this region has been attempted so far.

Very few historians have turned their attention to the study of the Southern Maratha County.

Many do not even know its exact location, for the simple reason that it has not been precisely defined so far. There is much ambiguity and confusion about the meaning and connotation of this term. About the political activities of the Marathas in this region (*i.e.*, Krishna-Tungabhadra Doab) some account has been found in certain works. But here too the reference is to notable Maratha leaders, and not to the local people. Again due to the non-availability of original archival documents relating to this region in the 17th century, especially during the Adilshahi period, its study of that period is largely neglected. In the published works on Bijapur, like those of Varma and Sinha, only a broad dutline of important political activities is given, which does not help us much in studying the political life of this region during that period. The *Shiva-Charitra-Sahitya*, No. 6 published by the Bharat Itihas Samshodhak Mandal, Pune, contains a number of original Persian and Modi papers throwing light on the Desais of Dharwad, Hubli, Gadag, Lakshmeshwar etc. The Bharat Itihas Samshodhak Mandal has also a number of Kannad documents relating to Lakshmeshwar Desais that flourished under the Adilshahs, and some of these papers deal with individual people in the principality of Lakshmeshwar Desais giving us a glimpse into the economic and social life of the people of those days in this region. As these papers are in Kannada and relate to this comparatively unknown region, they were not tapped by the researchers till I happened to study them.

The archival material available in the Pune Archives and to some extent in the Kolhapur Archives and the Bharat Itihas Samshodhak Mandal Archives are of greatest use for the economic study of this region during the Peshwa period. Most of them are in Modi and some in Kannada and very few in Persian. We have also a large number of original English documents in Pune and Bombay Archives, but they mostly belong to the Company's period. Yet they are of considerable use as they give us an idea of the economic conditions in the Maratha period immediately preceding the Company's period. In this regard the Revenue Settlement Report of Captain Wingate, Chaplin's Report, and the reports of other similar administrators are very informative and illuminating.

Mr. Langford's Report on the Konkan and Southern Maratha Country is very useful as throwing light on the Mohtarfa taxes in this region.

The Modi documents give minute details about the administrative system in this area, about the various administrative divisions, the number of villages in these divisions, the types of lands, the crops grown on the lands, the land measurements, various land tenures, the methods of collecting taxes, various types of taxes, patterns of land holding, the extent of proprietary rights in land enjoyed by different classes of cultivators, the agrarian relations between the state, landholders and cultivators including landless labourers, the extent of exploitation practised on the landless people and petty land-holders by the big watandars and administrative officers, the articles of trade, the trade routes, the prices of articles, various land transactions such as the lease of lands, sale of lands and mortgage of lands, money and banking transactions, and the like.

The archival documents consulted are of various types such as the Taleband, Dehzadas, Zaminzada, Thalzada, Yadast, Niwadpatra, Hiseb Beheda, Hukmnama, Jamabandi, Kaulnama, Istava, Kaifiyat, Lavni, Jabta Varshasane, Wasul Jamakharch, Kird, Ajnapatra, Jabita Wantane, Bhogyadi Patra, Krayapatra, Genealogy, Zadti, Nirupa, Yadi Dharmadav, Kabulayati Kagad, Rakmala, Terij, Nemunk Beheda, Bhudanapatra, Sanad, Akar Jamabandi, Terij Jamabandi, Terij Zaminzada, Terij Wasul Baqi, Ajmas Taluke, Taleband Ijmayli, Inamat, Parwana, Takid, Karjakhat, Mohtarfa Wasul, Sadilwarzada, Patrak Kularag, Wahiwat and so on. This will give us an idea of the rich variety and complexity of the archival source material available on the subject. It is not possible within the limited space here to deal with all the types of documents that are pressed into service for writing this monograph. However, a few specimens can be briefly explained.

The Taleband could be of three types, *viz.*, an yearly Taleband, a monthly Taleband and an Ijmayili Taleband. It is usually an yearly Taleband. It could also be a monthly Taleband forwarded by the district revenue officers to the government showing the receipts and disbursements of the preceding month, and the balance at its close. When it is an yearly Taleband, it gives a detailed account of the actual receipts and disbursements of the year, as well as of the outstanding balances at its beginning and at its close. The Ijmayili Taleband is a superficial account roughly prepared to answer immediate purposes. Such Talebands were usually drawn up for the territories recently conquered or when they were not fully settled. The second type of document is called the Wahiwat. The term "Wahiwat" means administration or management. It might also relate to the collection of revenue. It appears that the term was employed especially for the administration of a newly-acquired territory where the administrative system was not firmly established and where the tradition and custom played an important part. When used along with a Taleband, as in "Taleband Wahiwat of Taluka Savanur", it would mean a financial account, yearly, or monthly or Ijmayili, showing the receipts and disbursements effected mainly according to traditional rules and regulations or according to custom, although the introduction of the new administrative rules in some measure is generally not ruled out.

A *Yad* or *Yadi* is a memorandum, a scrap or a little account. It could also be an administrative catalogue of important items of accounts A Yadi of Masala (It could be a list of exactions levied under the Marathas on every person summoned to answer a charge against him) is a Yadi of fees payable to inferior native officers or messengers sent to collect the revenue. The Dehzada is an official document giving a catalogue of villages in a particular administrative division with revenue details. The Zabta or Zabita means a list or a roll or a descriptive catalogue of any items such as villages, grants, persons, gifts, donations or fees.[1]

Like the Dehzada, the Zaminzada is a catalogue of holdings that each peasant or proprietor or tenant had, showing the tenure under which he held his lands. This is a very important type of document, for it furnishes a complete picture of the pattern of landholding in a given village. From it we know the total extent of lands in a village, their distribution as waste lands, as lands under judicial enquiry, as *khalsa* or *wahati* lands, as Inam lands, watan lands and the rates of land tax. This also gives us a glimpse into the agrarian relations obtaining in the village and the accumulation of the surplus produce in some hands.

Beheda is a rough estimate of receipts and expenditure in a given revenue district, made on the basis of accounts papers of previous years. Such *Behedas* were utilised for granting the Kamavis (the right to collect revenue) to a candidate or for restoring a principality to its erstwhile chieftain. The Ajmas, like Beheda, is a document giving an estimate of the income and expenditure of a given revenue area like the Prant. If the *Behedas* were prepared mostly for bigger tracts such as principalities or desgats, the Prant Ajmases were prepared for the regular administrative divisions called Prants. This gives minute details of yearly account of Prants down to the smallest fractions of a rupee. The Jamabandi is a document giving the details of the settlement of land revenue. The *Rakmala* is a similar document giving the total rent collected for a given

1. Wilson's Glossary (Delhi, 1968), pp. 215, 333, 504, 553, 558.

year and the rates of revenue for different types of lands, *rakn* meaning the standard land tax. The *Kaulnama* is a lease of land on easy terms whereas *Istava* is a lease of lands for a fixed period of time, the rent payable being increased gradually year by year until it reaches the standard rent paid for other lands of the same type. The *Kaifiyat* is a document mostly belonging to the early Company's period resembling a questionnaire about a landholding or any other revenue matter eliciting information from the holder of the land about the original granter and grantee of the said land, the tax paid for it, the number of generations enjoying the land, confiscation of the land, if it had taken place, etc. Although it belongs to the early Company's period, it gives many valuable-details about the land system of the earlier days, sometimes even of the times of Aurangzeb. When corroborated by other documents this information really becomes very valuable and authentic. Deeds recording various land transactions such as sale, mortgage gift etc. are indicated by such terms as *Krayapatra, Bhogyadipatra, Danapatra* etc. Many of these documents, especially those giving revenue details, have their own abstracts called Terij which are very handy and give the whole picture at a glance.

Documents such as these are usually in the Marathi language and the Modi script. But as the region about which these documents are available was not a part of Maharashtra, but of Karnataka, often Kannada equivalents were given in the documents like *Kunbini-Vakkalagitti* or *poli-rotti* where both the words mean the same thing in two different languages. Sometimes the languages of the document would be Kannad and the script Modi. When both the script and language are in Kannada, especially for revenue documents, the Kannad language would be so full of Marathi and Persian revenue terms that one doubts it to be the Kannada language. This was the need of the hour, and both the administrators and the people of the region welcomed this sort of writing.

The Modi documents are found not only in the Pune, Bombay and Kolhapur Archives but also in the Karnataka Archives. There they are known as Manoli papers as most of them relate to Taluka Manoli or Munavalli.

The documents available in the Bharat Itihas Samshodhak Mandal enlighten us on private land and money transactions, and provide a good supplement to the information furnished by the documents of the above Government Archives. Some of these documents are of Adilshahi times, and provide a good background for the study of the revenue system under Shivaji and later under the Peshwas.

The Ramdurg Palace Daftar gives us documents that deal with only one state and serve as specimens of such types of papers. It also has a considerable amount of papers throwing light on the temple administration at the capital giving minute details about the temple employees and officials, income, expenditure etc. The Nargund Pujari Daftar contains a large number of Modi and some Kannada documents relating to the priestly family and its three branches settled at three different places, the family whose head had received a grant of lands from the Ramdurg chief for his services as a priest in the Venkateshwar temple at Nargund. These documents incidentally throw light on money transactions involving hundis or bills of exchange, etc. It is in one of these documents that I first came to know that one *mar* of land (a term which was used in Vijaynagara times) was later on equivalent to 36 bighas.

Thus all these documents which are a mine of authentic historical information and the published original material supply a firm base for the reconstruction of the political, social and economic history of the Krishna-Tungabhadra Doab, later known as the Southern Maratha Country.

As regards the authenticity and credibility of these sources, it can be said that the administrative documents such as Talebands, Zaminzadas, Gaonzadas, Yadis, Behedas and the like are, as a rule, both authentic and credible. As they were administrative papers, generally nobody tampered with them. Again we often find several copies of the document as they were to be sent to different persons for information and action. Usually the original document was corroborated by these copies. In respect of Kaifiyats, one may note that they are authentic like the administrative papers, and the contents are generally credible, for in many cases the contents are supported by the original documents attached to them. The terms used in these documents are of the Peshwa times or even of earlier times, and mostly they are found to be correct and genuine. Of course, if the *Bakhars* are used, then one has to be very cautious, for they were written at a later date and the author had every opportunity to insert into them his own ideas or information. However, here no *bakhars* are used, as they are not available at all for this area and for this period. Hence only the authentic and credible sources have been used for writing this book.

II

Administrative Systems

Administrative Divisions

Under the Mughals Bijapur became one of the 6 Deccan Subas, and it was divided for administrative purposes into 18 Sarkars which were like districts. These were (1) Haveli Bijapur, (2) Miraj, (3) Azamnagar, (4) Panhala, (5) Kaibag, (6) Malikwad, (7) Karnataka, (8) Bankapur, (9) Torgal, (10) Gazipur, 11) Adawani, 12) Mudgal, (13) Sagar, (14) Raichur, (15) Dabhol, (16) Naldurg, (17) Malkhed, and (18) Gulbarga[1].

In the contemporary Modi documents available Azamnagar, Bankapur and Torgal are often mentioned as Sarkars coming in this area, and Bijapur is mentioned as a Suba. The term 'Subha' meaning a province or a bigger administrative division than the Pargana, was in the early days exclusively used for Bijapur only. Thus a document form the Karnatak Jamav of the Peshwa Daftar[2] dated 1680 says that Sarkar Bankapur was in the Subhe Darul-Jafar Bijyapur. Even as late as 1755 it was mentioned as a Subah[3]. But from 1706 onwards one finds other names of places competing with Bijapur for the coveted nomenclature of Subha. In 1706-07 Belgaum, Lakshmeshwar, Sampagaon, Nargund and Navalgund were also called Subhas.[4] In 1714 Hukkeri was raised to the status of the Subah.[5]

The next term that is met with in administrative matters is 'Prant'. From a study of the context in which this term was used in various

1. Pune Archives, Karnatak Jamav, Rumal No. 1938, serial No. 691.
2. *Ibid.*, 170 : 170.
3. A.G. Pawar (ed.) *Tarabaikalina Kagadapture*, 3:94.
4. *TKK*: 1: 185.
5. *Ibid.*, 1: 291.

documents, one feels that it was loosely used for an area where all the territories were not fully brought under Maratha sway, but where the Maratha hegemony was imposed, only some. Parganas having been brought under control. Generally the saranjams or the alienated villages were included in the Prant. Such were the Prants of Gadag, Koppal, Hukkeri, Bankapur, Karnatak, Kittur, and Miraj. It must be noted that each one of these divisions was used for a different administrative unit such as Pargana, or Taluka or Suba. But here the term Prant is used in a different sense for a specific purpose.

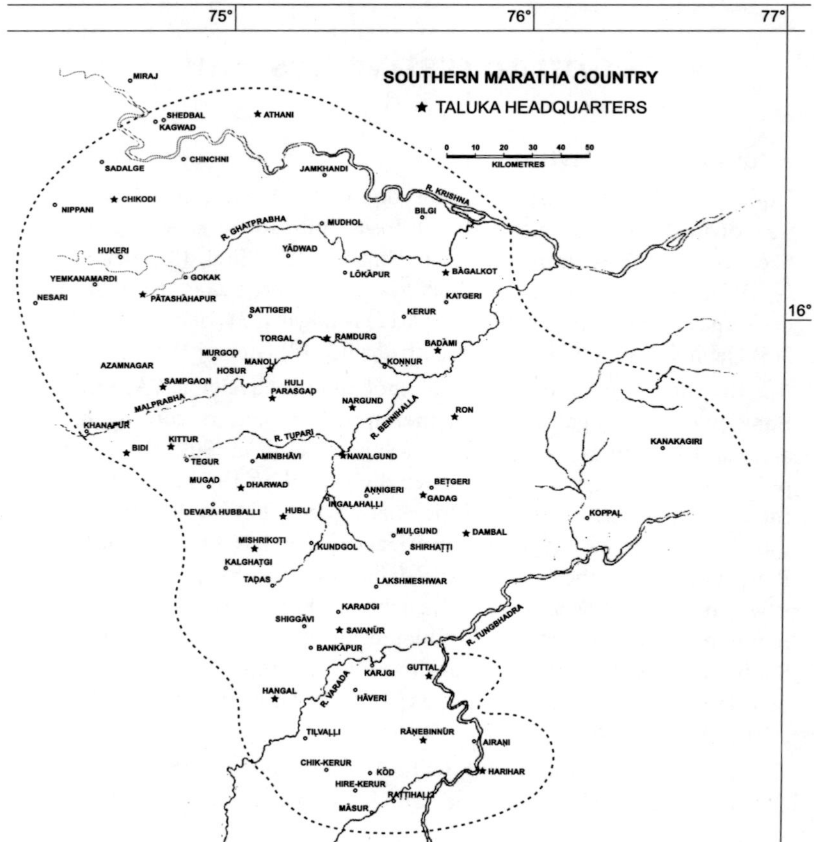

Next Hukkeri is often mentioned as a Prant. There is a significant reason for this. The area between the Ghatprabha and the Tungabhadra was included for a long time in the kingdom of the Nawabs of Savanur, while the area between the Ghataprabha and the Krishna often changed hands. Although the Nawabs of Savanur did rule over this area for some time, yet parts of it came under Maratha sway. It was, as it were, a "No Man's Land." Especially, the chiefs of Kapshi had many jagirs here. It was always a bone of contention between the Peshwas and the Kolhapur Chhatrapatis. Places like Iat, Eksambe, Manoli and Hukkeri itself were under the Kapshi chiefs. A document, for example, of 1703 says that the mokasa of Karyati Prant Hukkeri was with Piraji Ghorpade[1]. In 1734 Sambhaji II of Kolhapur could grant in inam the village of Hanaminihal in Karyat Nul of Prant Hukkeri to Baburao Janoji Nalavade.[2] On the other hand in 1763 Madhavrao I ordered Basava Prabhu Desai of Prant Hukkeri to hand over to Aisaheb (of Kolhapur) the thanas of Chikkodi, Bage wadi and Vantamuri[3]. In 1766 Prant Hukkeri 'consisted of nine qasbas, *viz.*, (1) Kabbur, (2) Manoli, (3) Jugolgaon, (4) Nejgaon, (5) Savgaon, (6) Lat, (7) Sadalge, (8) Manati and (9) Hukkeri.[4]

There were three other administrative units, *viz.*, Qasba, Pethand Hisar. The Qasba was the most important place of the Pargana, and usually its headquarters. It was a semi-urban centre. The Peth was an urban centre, having a different type of population, performing non-agricultural professions. There were very few Peths such as Haveri, Havasbhavi and Majidpur or Hubli. The Hisars were forts, and the places called Hisars here were or had once been mainly known for their strong forts, and hence the term was continued in such cases. Besides the Hisars, there were many places, generally the headquarters and administratively important places, which had forts. In such cases there used to be a separate commandant in charge of the forts, who was usually not responsible to the Pargana Officer, but to the central Government. The administrative pattern in these forts was different from that in the Parganas. These became in course of time the nuclii of urban centres. In England the boroughs developed out of the burghs, which were forts. These were the nuclii of urban centres, having a different system of administration. Some of these, of course, became rotten boroughs later on, especially when new urban centres grew up in the wake of industrial revolution. One finds a similar phenomenon here in different sets of administrative officers for the fort administration and for the Pargana administration.

---

1. *TKK*: 1: 142
2. 2S.M. Garge (cd.), *Karavir Riyasatichi Kagadapatre*, 1: 3; Nivadi: 1276.
3. *Ibid.*, 1: 15, Nivadi: 65.
4. KJ: 349: 311.

In Shivaji's times there were eight divisions called Prants in the Southern Maratha Country. These Prants were (1) Belgaum-Patshapur, (2) Sampgaon, (3) Gadag, (4) Lakshmeshwar, (5) Navalgund, (6) Koppal, (7) Betgeri, and (8) Halyal. These are called Mahals, which would suggest that they were revenue-paying units, and not administrative divisions. Although these Mahals were within the Krishna-Tungabhadra Doab, they did not cover the whole area of the Doab. For example, Nippani, Chikkodi, Hukkeri, Athani and Raibag in the north, while Ranebennur, Hirekerur and Harihar in the south were not covered. But these were mostly included in the administrative divisions formed by the Adilshahs, from whose territories the tribute was collected by Shivaji. The Savanur Nawabs had organised this area into the earlier three divisions called Sarkars. These were Sarkar Azamnagar or Belgaum in the north, Sarkar Torgal in the centre and Sarkar Bankapur in the south. Sarkar Azamnagar included 16 Parganas of which Hukkeri, Gokak, Kapshi, and Lat were in the north.[1] About the same time (A.D. 1680) Sarkar Bankapur in the south contained 16 Parganas, covering Masur, Rattehalli, Harihar and Honnali in the extreme south. All these three sarkars were in Subha Bijapur. Although the terms like Sarkar Bankapur and Torgal and Subha Bijapur were used long afterwards in the documents, this area under the Peshwas came to be known as Prant Karnatak divided into a number of Talukas which were regular administrative divisions. The talukas in Prant Karnatak as mentioned in the documents of the Peshwa period were : (1) Athani, (2) Chikkodi, (3) Kittur, (4) Mudakavi, (5) Badami, (6) Manoli, (7) Ramdurg, (8) Nargund, (9) Navalgund, (10) Nandawadi, (11) Dharwad, (12) Gadag, and (13) Savanur.

It is surprising to note that none of the three Sarkar headquarters, namely, Azamnagar, Torgal and Bankapur, was made a taluka place under the Peshwas. The reason for this was obvious. Many villages round about Azamnagar were under the Patwardhans of Sangli, while Torgal and the neighbouring areas were under the Shindes of Torgal or the Chhatrapatis of Kolhapur. Bankapur was probably thrust into the background by the rise of Savanur as a Taluka place.

Jagirs and Desgats

Although the Krishna-Tungabhadra Doab was organised, for administrative purposes, into 13 talukas, they were all of them not directly under the Peshwa administration. Some like Athani and Savanur were directly administered by the Peshwas through their regularly

1. KJ: 270 : 170.

appointed administrators called Kamavisdars or Mamledars. Others were under the administration of Jagirdars to whom these talukas were entrusted. Such were, for example, Venkatrao Narayan of Ichalkaranji to whom was assigned the Dharwad taluka after its capture by the Peshwa from the Mughals in 1753. Similarly Ramdurg and Nargund were under their own chiefs, the Bhaves, but these were controlled by the Peshwa and the centre.

A number of territories in this area were held by the Patwardhans, Ghorpades and Rastes. Some were held by the Jagirdars of the Chatrapati of Kolhapur. And even in those territories that were directly administered by the Peshwas, some of the villages or parts of villages were held by the local Watandars such as Desais and Nadgaudas. Thus the people in this Doab were under the administration of different rulers. The area did not form one single whole administered by only one government.

Among the Patwardhans, the chieftains of Sangli, Miraj, Tasgaon, Jamkhandi, Kurundwad, Kagwad or Shedbal had their jagirs in the Doab. The Chief of Sangli held Terdal Pargana, Shirhatti Pargana, Shahapur Pargana and Dodwad Thana. The Lakshmeshwar Pargana of 15 villages belonged to the Chief of Miraj Sr. The Chief of Miraj Jr. held 15 villages in Gudgeri Mahal near Lakshmeshwar PetaTikote (Khatav) consisting of 2 villages in the later Kaladgi district west of Bijapur belonged to the Chief of Kurundwad Sr., while Yelur Taluka of 17 villages near Belgaum was under the Chief of Kurundwad Jr. In addition, the latter held 2 villages in Athani and Chikodi Talukas. The Jamkhandikars had almost all of their jagirs in the Doab. They included 39 villages in Peta Jamkhandi, 22 villages in Peta Bidri, 20 villages in Peta Kundgol and some villages in Belgaum area.

The Ghorpades of Mudhol ruled over the divisions of Mudhol, Dhavaleshwar, Machikanur, Jambagi and Lokapur all in the northern part of the Doab. All these divisions contained 79 villages.

The Sonikars, that is, the chiefs of the third branch of Miraj held Byahatti near Dharwad while the chiefs of the fourth branch of Miraj held 10 villages in Belgaum area and 8 villages in Dharwad area. The Rastes had a number of jagirs in Bagalkot, Hungund and Badami areas.

Alongside of these Talukas, and Samsthans there were independent and semi-independent petty local chiefs having their own jagirs or desgats. Such were, for example, the chiefs, of Kittur, Navalgund, Shirhatti, Lakshmeshwar, Havanur, Dambal, Nargund, Ramdurg, Nippani, Torgal, Mudhol and Athani. These chiefs enjoyed varying degrees of independence and power. The Nawabs of Savanur, the chiefs of Nargund and Ramdurg, the Desais of Kittur and Nippani and the Chiefs of Athani were among the powerful chieftains owing only a nominal allegiance to the Peshwa. Sardesais had Sardesgats as their watans. The Sardesai and Sarnadgauda were similar hereditary officials in charge of slightly bigger areas. At the village level were the Gaudas and Kulkarnis or Shanbhogs, the village counterparts of the Nadgauda or Sardesai and Sardeshpande. Kamavisdars were appointed in charge of Parganas or Samats.

Administrative Officers

After discussing the administrative framework with its divisions, we shall now note a few details about the actual office-bearers who held these posts.

Abdul Karim Bahlol Khan was the administrator for the area of the above three Sarkars. After him the Nawabs of Savanur, the successors of Abdul Karim, became the rulers of this area, except a small portion to the north of the Ghataprabha. This portion was always in an unsteady position. For some time it was included in the principalities of the Kapshi chiefs and the Kolhapur Chhatrapatis.

After the conquest of most of this area from the Nawabs of Savanur and from some other local chiefs by the Peshwas, this Doab was made a big administrative unit or province called Suba Karnatak and a governor was appointed for its administration. During Shivaji's and Rajaram's times, Ramchandra Pant Amatya seems to have been the governor in charge of this area. When it went under the sway of the Peshwas, they appointed a Sarsubhedar over Prant/Suba Karnatak. Thus we know that in 1764 Moro Bapuji was appointed Sarsubha of Prant Karnataka[1] and that in 1775 Yeshwantrao Shinde was the Sarsubhedar.[2] In 1787 Lakshman Baburao is found in charge of Prant Karnatak[3]. The Sarsubhedar was often mentioned as Sarsubha or Subha only, using the short form of the former term. Already by 1804, Trimabakji Dengle was in charge of Prant Karnatak.[4] In 1808, however, there was a break in the governorship of Trimbakji Dengle for sometime. For, in that year we find Anandrao Ramchandra functioning as Sarsubha of Prant Karnatak.[5] But

1. G.C. Vad (ed.), *Selections from Satara Raja's and Peshwas' Diaries*, 8/3; 849.
2. Bharat Itihas Samshodhak Mandal Archives, No. 47
3. KJ: 554 : 393.
4. KJ: 554 : 429.
5. KJ: 232 : 642.

Dengle managed to get back his governorship of Karnatak[1] in 1813 and continued to be in that post till the fall of the Peshwa Government in 1818.

After the Prant, the next smaller, but regular administrative division, was the taluka, of which there were, as mentioned earlier, 13 in Prant Karnatak. There were regular officers appointed in charge of these talukas, called Kamavisdars or Mamlatdars. For example, in 1793 Abaji Baburao was the Kamavisdar of Taluka Kittur[2], while in 1795 Mahadji Khanderao was its Kamavisdar.[3] In 1764 Madhavarao Krishna was in charge of Taluka Mudakavi, Govind Bhikaji in charge of Taluka Navalgund, Anandrao Ramchandra in charge of Taluka Gadag, Balarao Yeshwant in charge of Taluka Dharwad, and Mahadji Khanderao in charge of Taluka Kittur.[4]

Pattanasettis were appointed in charge of Peths, and commandants in charge of forts and qasbas. Thus Bapuji Shinde was the commandant of the Dharwad fort.[5]

Similarly for the fort of Belgaum also there was a commandant. Between January 1799 and October 1815 there were as many as 9 commandants of Kille Belgaum, namely, Siddheshwar Mahipatrao, Dhondo Narayan, Balkrishna Lakshman, Keshavrao Balkrishna, Anandrao Ramchandra, Baburao Anant, Trimbakji Dengle, Parashram Khanderao and Wamanji Govind.[6]

Various elements in the administrative system

In the beginning the revenue administration in North Karnataka was largely modelled on the indigenous system such as was prevalent under Vijayanagara and Chalukyas of Kalyana, but gradually it came under Maratha influence when the Marathas began to extend their sway over Karnataka. Thus in 1586 we find the indigenous system prevalent here. A sale deed dated 1586 A.D. (written in Kannada) records the sale of one-fourth of the income of the office of Senabova (village accountant) by one Kalasappa of Balehosur to Lingana Gauda of Mantur. The date is given in the Salivahana Saka as 10th day of the dark half (bahula) of the month of Kartika belonging to the year of Vyaya of Saka 1508. Balehosur was part

1. KJ: 554 : 523.
2. KJ: 325 : 67.
3. *Ibid.*, 324 : 93
4. *SSRPD*: 8/3 : 849.
5. *SSRPD*: 7/2 : 660.
6. KJ: 270 : 169.

of the *sime* of Guttal. The sale deed is called Krayapatra, and the office of the village accountant was known as *Senabovike*. The perquisites of the Senabova included the *layamanya*, grass and fodder, and *maggavana*. Layamanya probably meant rent-free land granted for the maintenance of his horses and *maggavana* was a tax on looms. The one-fourth of the *Senabovike* was expressed in terms of varahas as 30 varahas.[1]

After the lapse of half a century we find the Maratha influence making itself felt in the Karnatak administration. Although the Hindu style of giving the date is retained, although there are still Kannada and Sanskrit revenue terms used, yet one comes across Marathi or Persian nomenclature making its appearance.

In 1640 Mahanayakacharya Baguli Basavappa Nayaka Areyya made a grant of some villages including a number of perquisites to Lakshmeshwar Desai Khanappa Gauda. Khanappa Gauda is said to have been the Desai of the sime of the Lakshmeshwar Pargana. Here it is interesting to notice that both the Kannada and Persian nomenclatures are used to denote the same administrative or revenue division. Formerly it was known as the Lakshmeshwar sime only, but now it was called the sime of the Lakshmeshwar Pargana. Again he is said to have been the Nadgauda of Kille Koppal and Pargana Rayara Hubli. Both Koppal and Rayara Hubli are described as simes. The Mudgal Sarkar is said to have been in the Koppal Prant. As the document alludes to the raids (lit. menace) of the Mughals and Marathas, here called Ares, the Persian influence must have made its way here either through the Mughals or through the Marathas. Mahanayakacharya Baguli Basavappa Nayaka enjoyed the Mirasi of the Nadgaudki in the Sime of Yelburgi. Mirasi, a Persian term, is used along with Nadgaudki, a Kannada word. The sowing capacity method is described as the Bijawari system which is a Kannada expression. The unit of the land measurement in North Karnataka in later days seems to be more akin to that of Maharashtra than to that of Vijayanagara. In Vijayanagara the measuring rod seems to have been originally based on the length of the foot of some ruler whereas in Maharashtra it seems to have been based on the measurements of fingers or knuckles or hands. Thus the *Shivashahi Kathi* was 5 cubits and 5 fists long[2] and Mar, a land measure used in North Karnataka, was, like the Kurgi or Nivartana in Maharashtra, indicative of the area that could be ploughed by two bullocks in a given period.

1. BISMA, L.D., 343.
2. A cubit was equal to 14 *tansus* and a fist was equal to 2 *tansus*.

Baguli Basavappa Nayaka also made a grant of some taxes and cesses, and a few of these were borrowed from the Marathas. The cesses mentioned here are those on *tambaku* (tobacoo), *ganigar yenne* (oil), *hadidi, hasike, pasike* (a handful of food-grains) *palige* (a spoonful or ladleful of oil), *kanthavanada vartane* (the village accountant's perquisites) *soppe* (fodder) etc. Here *pasike* and *palige* are clearly Marathi words, and must have been directly borrowed from the administrative system in Maharashtra. These were called *hakkalajima*, a Persian word commonly used in Maharashtra meaning 'rights and perquisites.'[1] *Muttalika* and *Kamavisa* are some other Persian revenue terms presumably borrowed from Maharashtra.

In 1655 we find a further development in the influence of the Maratha administration on that of Karnataka. A Kannada document dated A.D. 1655 records the mortgage transactions between a grandson of Timmaji Nayaka, the Gauda of Kasbe Sirguppi and Kenchanagauda, son of the Lakshmeshwar Desai Khanappa Gauda. It speaks of the *judi-manya*, *i.e.* quit-rent (judi) levied on a piece of land granted originally as an inam land (*manya*). This is similar to the *dumale* inam lands in Maharashtra. An important feature of this mortgage deed (*bhogavatiya-patra*) is that it bears the signature of the mortgagor in the Devanagari script.

In 1679 a document recording a mortgage deed bears the attestation mark of the Gauda along with his signature — a clear instance of the direct borrowing of revenue administrative features from Maharashtra, for in Karnataka, unlike in Maharashtra, no village official or servant put his attestation mark on the document. A second feature of this document which shows the increasing influence of the Maratha administration on North Karnataka is the method of starting the year. So far the year of the transaction was given only in the Salivahana Saka, but now along with the Salavahana Saka the Fasli year also is given as Tissa Sabain Alaf. In 1688 we find the Fasli year given both in words and figures. From a document of 1691, we know how a farman was given bestowing the Desgat on the donee, how the *khalsati* as against *umali* (Inam) lands were granted and how along with the villages *chavarati vartane*, *tainati*, *tashrifu* and the *Inamati* village were made over. Small villages were called, as in Maharashtra, Majares, and the market places Kasbas.

In 1794 we find the revenue administration in Southern Maratha Country acquiring striking similarity to that of Maharashtra, which is

1. BISM Archives, LD 42.

given expression to in the Yadi of Kille Dharwad. The style is Maratha, but the contents relate to Karnataka. Although the script is Kannad, 80% of the words are Marathi or Persian. It starts as "Yadi Kille Dharwad Nisbat Bapuji Shinde Sur San Arba Tisain Maya va Allaf". The Yadi enumerates the names of the officials of the fort, their salaries and other items for which money was earmarked. The officials included:

1. Bapuji Shinde, the Killedar,
2. Bapurao Havaldar,
3. Kedarji Pawar Sarnaubat,
4. Haibatrao Shankar Karkhanis,
5. Janardan Lakshman Daptardar Nisbat Hashmnis, etc.

The amount assigned to some of these officers was to cover the expenses on palanquin beares (*palikki* bovi), the batman (*Huduga*, in Marathi *porga*) etc.

The next item of expenditure was on the garrison here called Shibandi, as in Maharashtra. The assignments covered the salaries (*rojmara*) of the Tainat Hawaldar, of the Gardis, of the *Golandaz* (gunners), of the *Janjala* (camel gun), of the Bandars (Archers), of the cavalry-men (swar), etc. Besides, various sums were to be spent in continuing the traditional grants to various institutions, and on other items continued from the previous year. Such were the grants to temples (Devasthana), for the Dasara expenses, for the Dipawali expenses, for the illumination expenses (*rosana*), for the office expenses (*daptar-kharch*), for the celebration of the first day of the year (*shimga-kharch*), for the Ganesh Chaturthi expenses, for the 2nd day of bright fortnight expenses (*Chandarat*), for the expenses of the maid-servant (*Kunabini-Vakkalagitti*). Here *Kunabini* is a Marathi word and Vakkalagitti a Kannada word, both meaning the same thing, but used together as one word, probably because the common people did not know the meaning *Kunabini* and that it was being introduced recently in Kannada revenue records. Some amounts were sanctioned according to the *beheda, i.e.*, the annual estimate of income and expenditure.

SOME EXAMPLES

Kittur Principality

The Kittur principality which flourished in the 17th and 18th centuries included some portions of the present Belgaum and Dharwad districts.

It was actually founded by Allappaguada Sardesai (1650-81), although four of his predecessors including the progenitor of this dynasty Hiremallasetti, were serving in this area under the Bijapur Adilshahs. After Allappaguda seven rulers ruled over Kittur till 1824. After the fall of Bijapur in 1686, when Allappagauda's successor Mudimallappa was ruling, for one year from 1686-87, the administration of the Kittur principality was carried on by the Savanur Nawab Rauf Khan. Thereafter till 1747 the Kittur Desais seem to have been under the Nawabs of Savanur. In 1747 the Pargana of Sampgaon-Kittur was one of the 35 *Mahals* surrendered to Balaji Bajirao Peshwa by Abdul Majid Khan, the Nawab of Savanur by a treaty concluded between them.[1] At this time Malavarudragauda, the fifth from Allappagauda, was the chief of Kittur. Only two years after this treaty, that is in 1749, Virappagauda succeeded him as the chief, and it was with Virappagauda that the Marathas came in closer contact. Virappagaudda was ruling over Parasgad, Sampgaon, Bidi and other areas. Although Sampgaon-Kittur were surrendered to Balaji Bajirao in 1747, it appears that Virappa Mallappagauda was ruling over Mamla Hubli and other areas in the capacity of a feudatory chief paying some tribute to the Peshwa. In 1753-54 Virappagauda was compelled to pay a tribute of 80,000 rupees to the Peshwa Govt, through Lingo Appaji, this time mainly for meeting the expenses incurred by the Peshwa when his troops were engaged in an attack in this area.[2] In 1778 Virappagauda occupied Gokak which was under the Peshwa, but was defeated in 1779 by Parashuram Bhau sent by the Peshwa against the Desai.[3] Virappagauda was succeeded by Mallappa (gauda) in 1782. This was a crucial date in the history of the Southern Maratha Country as well as of North India. In this year the Treaty of Salbai was concluded bringing to a close the First Anglo-Maratha War in the north, while in the south Hyder Ali was succeeded by his son Tipu Sultan. Hyder Ali who had been a party to the Anti-British Confederacy organised mainly by Nana Phadnis during the First Anglo-Martha War, was not consulted for concluding the Treaty of Salbai. Feeling highly offended and humiliated, Hyder Ali launched a widespread and highly organised aggression against the Maratha territories in Karnataka. After his death in the same year his son Tipu continued these aggressive activities in a more violent manner, seized Badami, Nargund and Kittur, overrunning the Doab between the

1. *Dilerjangi*, p. 18; *Taha va Kararmadar*, p. 86.
2. *SSRPD*. III, p. 148.
3. *Bom. Gaz.*, Vol. 21, p. 579.

Malaprabha and the Ghataprabha. In 1785, Kittur fell and Mallasarjya, its ruler, was taken prisoner by Tipu. But the Marathas retrieved this loss very soon and in 1787 the Gajendragad Treaty was concluded by which Tipu surrendered, among other principalities and places, Kittur to the Marathas. On its surrender, the Maratha Govt. appointed Baburao Bhaskar as an officer in charge of Kittur. From now onwards the Kittur principality mostly remained under the Marathas, except for some time after 1814. The Kittur Chief was turned into a Zamindar (jagirdar) giving him a jagir of just 11 villages. These villages were (1) Hunashikatti, (2) Hosur (both in Karyat Kadarvali), (3) Itagi, (4) Gandigwad, (5) Badas (all the three in Karyat Phutgaon), (6) Hongal (in Karyat Belvadi), (7) Tigadi (in Karyat Sampgaon), (8) Sutagatti (in Karyat Nesari), (9) Devalati (in Karyat Lokoli), (10) Degaon (in Karyat Ambadgatti), and (11) Devara-Sigihalli (in Karyat Phutgaon) (KJ : 325 : 1).

It appears that in 1747, after taking Kittur-Sampgaon from the Nawab of Savanur by a treaty, Nana Saheb appointed an officer in charge of the Kittur area, although at present we do not know the name of this officer. In 1764, however, the officer in charge of Taluka Kittur was Mahadaji Khanderao when Moro Bapuji was the Sarsubha of Prant Karnatak.[1] In 1782, as noted above, Baburao Bhaskar was the officer in charge of Taluka Kittur. In 1792-93 the Mamlat of Kittur was under Abaji Baburao,[2] probably the son of Baburao Bhaskar. At this time Taluka Kittur was organised for administrative purposes into 14 Karyats. It may be noted that in the Modi document[3] Karlakatti is mentioned as Karalge, Lokoli as Kekholi, Ambadagatti as Amargate, Kakkeri as Kalori and Godholi as Golehalli.

In 1794 Mahadaji Khanderao was the Mamledar of Kittur Taluka. In 1814, however, the administration of Taluka Kittur including Mamla Hubli and other Mahals (Kittur Desgat) was entrusted by the Peshwa to Mallasarja.[4]

A document of A. D. 1793[5] speaks of the earlier administration of Taluka Kittur by Anandrao Ramchandra who seems to have immediately preceded Abaji Baburao. It also says that earlier the Kamavisdar was

1. *SSRPD*. VIII, No. 849, pp. 25-27.
2. Decan College Historical Museum, Rumal No. 74, File No. 10, Paper No. 2.
3. Pune Archives, Karnatak Jamav, Rumal No. 325. More details of the contents of this document are given in the sequel.
4. KJ: 324.
5. *Ibid*.

Balaji Trimal. Of the four Modi documents dealt with in this connection, the first is dated 1793, the second and the third are Talebands, dated A. D. 1794 and the last one is dated 1820. The second is a memorandum (Pune Archives, Karnatak Jamav, Rumal No. 325) of Taluka Kittur. In the beginning itself the memorandum says that the Mamlat of this Taluka was earlier with Abaji Baburao, and that in this year (1794) only he was replaced by Mahadaji Khanderao.

The document gives the revenue collection of this year Karyat-wise as follows: Kadarvali 6488-1-0, Kekoli 4014-6-2, Nesari 6741-9-2, Begevadi 1563-0-0, Halasi 6899-1-0, Nandgad 3817-0-0, Karalge 5528-11-0, Amargate 12292-12-2, Peth Kittur 4869-8-0, Phutgaon 7577-0-1, Manoli 6785-9-2, Golehalli 4418-10-1, Sampgaon 29409-8-0, Belvadi 12035-6-0, and Qasba Hubli 5873-0-1.

In Taluka Kittur there were a number of Zamindars to whom the lands (or land revenue) were alienated, and Mallappa Virappagauda Desai of Kittur was just one of them. From the alienated villages held by Mallasarja, a sum of Rs. 15,818-9-2 was realised as revenue. The villages alienated to him were Mangaon (in Karyat Chandgad), Tigadi (in Karyat Sampgaon), Hanabarhatti (in Karyat Sardesgat), Hosakote (in Karyat Sardesgat), Itagi, Ranakude (in Paragana Shahpur), Bastavad (in Pargana Shahpur), Hosur (in Karyat Kadarvali), Hunasikatte (in Karyat Kadarvali), Sampgaon (Patilki) (in Pargana Shahpur), Sardesgat (in Pargana Khanapur), Kamat Balegaon, and some other villages.

The custom duties amounting to Rs. 460-3-2 were realised from Peth Kittur, Kekoli, Karyat Nesari, Karyat Halasi, Nandgad and Karyat Sampgaon

The Siway-Jama and Kamavis brought in an amount of Rs. 2517-15-2. Under this head *Nazar-bhet* (presents) and masala (fees to minor revenue officials) were included. *Nazar-bhet* and *masala* were collected from Karyat Amargate, Karyat Nandgad, Karyat Halasi, Karyat Sampgaon, Karyat Kekoli, Mauje Rankude and Bastavad in Pargana Khanapur, Qasba Hubli, Karyat Golehalli, Karyat Karalgi, Karyat Balevadi (Belavadi), Mauje Akale in Karyat Bagewadi, Karyat Kadarvali, Karyat Nesari, Karyat Manoli and Karyat Futgaon.

Under Kamavis which was a joint head with Siway-Jama collections from judicial fees (Khanda-gunhegari), *batta* and *kasar* were included.

The total revenue realized from Taluka Kittur for the year 1794 came to be Rs. 1,37,976-0-1 as shown below:

(A) 1,34,047-13-1	Original Jama from various villages included under different Karyats, including 19,234-9-2 from Zamindars like Desai, etc. and 145-0-0 from Inamat.
(B) 460-3-3	From Zakat or customs dues
(C) 2517-15-2	From Siway-Jama and Kamavis
(D) 950-0-0	Arrears of the previous year
Rs. 1,37,976-0-1	Total revenue.

The heads of expenditure included salaries to the Mamledar, Darkdars, to the Gardis of the Peshwa who had been despatched to Dharwad for putting down a local riot, to Karkuns, etc.:

(A) Rs 6858 were paid to Mahadaji Khanderao Mamledar, of which 6000 constituted the basic pay, and 858 the Palanquin allowance.

(B) The Darakdars who received the salaries were as under:

Amount of Salary per year (In Rs).		*Name of Darkdar*
1. 433	—	Balavantrao Siddheswar Majamdar
2. 421	—	Krishnaji Sadashiv Phandnis
3. 250	—	Balaji Govind Daftardar

(C) Salaries yet to be sanctioned.

4. 1373	—	Gardis in the service of Balaji Vithal
5. 342	—	-do- Jafar Beg
6. 840	—	-do- Muse Khan
7. 575	—	-do- Sidi Mubarak

(D) Temporary Darkdars appointed on *adhoc* basis as the regular Darakdars could not join their duties, were as follows

8. 361-4-0	—	Ramchandra Balal Hashamnis
9. 214-8-0	—	Visaji Narayan Phadnis under *Hasham*
10. 171-8-0	—	Janardan Ramchandra Daftardar under *Hasham*
11. 171-8-0	—	Dhondo Govind Potnis
12. 85-12-0	—	Mahadaji Balal Karkun

(E) Besides, the Mamledar appointed some Karkuns, exercising his discretionary powers, for some specific purposes. These were the following :

13. 1057-8-0 Venkaji Ramchandra, (14) 257-8-0 Bapuji Ramchandra, (15) 342-0-0 Hari Govind, (16) 257-8-0 Damodar Baburao, (17) 428-0-0 Govind Balal, (F) Karkuns employed for helping the Phadnis, (18) 300-0-0 Keso Krishna, (19) 200-0-0 Anandrao Krishna, (G) Tarafdar Karkuns employed for work in the Karyats, (20) 64-0-0 Venkaji Hari, (21) 58-4-0 Naro Balal, (22) 63-8-0 Sivram Anant, (23) 57-0-0- Ramchandra Narahar, (24) 114-0-0-Rajaram Vasudev, (25) 80-0-0 Bhivrao Subarao, (26) 54-0-0 Ganesh Govind, (27) 151-8-0 Babaji Chimnaji, (28) 85-12-0 More Ramchandra, (29) 84-0-0 Bhivrao Sripat, (30) 107-0-0- Venkaji Bhikaji, (31) 213-8-0 Sadasiv Chimnaji (32) 79-0-0- Abaji Malhar, (33) 64-4-0 Bapuji Bhikaji (34) 156-4-0 Gopal Devaji, (35) 190-0-0 Govind Balal, (36) 35-12-0 Abaji Jagannath, (37) 172-8-0 Sakha Devrao, (38) 26-8-0 Chaudapa Naik, (39) 149-8-0 Ganesh Balal, (40) 79-0-0 Bhaskar Krishna, (41) 39-8-0 Moro Sakharam. Different sums were paid to many others as their salaries.

The administration of the Taluka of Kittur seems, from a perusal of the above list, to have been carried on mainly by the Marathi officers including mostly Brahmins and also a few Marathas and Muslims. Only one official, namely, Chaudapa Nayaka, seems to have been employed from among the local people.

Taluka Kittur was under Maratha administration for some years. In 1793, of which year we have a Taleband, Abaji Baburao was in charge of this taluka which consisted of one Kasba and 14 Karyats. The Kasba was Hubli (*i.e.* Mugutkhan Hubli), and the Karyats were Belvadi, Sampagaon, Halsai, Karalge, Kekholi, Nesari, Golehalli, Amargate, Manoli, Nandgad, Kadarvali, Phutgaon, Kalori and Bagewadi. These Karyats consisted of 2824 villages. These villages together with the Hubli Kasba formed 285 Mahals or revenue-paying units of Taluka Kittur. Of these, 11 villages were inam villages granted to Chintamanrao Pandurang Mirajkar, Daulatarao Ghorpade of Killa Hanmantgad, Sripatrao Sardeshpande, Bhupatrao Desai, Naro Deshpande, Rudrappa Desai, Rudro Virupaksh Kulkarni and Gurappa Desai.

22 villages were given in saranjam to Raghunathrao Nilkanth Kurundwadkar.

2 villages were given in *kamavis* to Siddheshwarrao Mahipat Binivale.

21 were Dumale villages under Mallappa Virappagauda Sardesai.

1 was under Bhimaji Baburao.

44 were under Bishtappa Desai Kalorekar.

Out of 285 Mahals 91 were thus either Inam or Saranjam Kamavis or Dumali villages and the remaining 194 villages were under the Maratha Government. From these villages Rs. 410786-0-9 were received as revenue consisting of land revenue, sadhanuk, *Ainat* and *Kharchapatti*. It seems that the revenue was collected under seven standard heads, *viz. Jamabandi, Pavalapatti, Ainat, Jajatipatti, Sadhanuk* and *Kharchapatti.*

Besides the above amount, a sum of Rs. 4516-10-0 was collected as extra revenue. Rs. 8612-8-0 were received as Nazar from Inamdars. Another sum was received from watandars, Judidars and Kamavisdars.

The above is a abroad classification of sources of income. The various particular sources of income included Chaval-palti, Gudipatti and the like.[1]

Paval-patti seems to have been a cess levied at the rate of 4 annas per rupee of the original land assessment. Thus the cess levied on 26-8-0 comes to 6-10-0. *Chavala-patti* was probably levied at the rate of 2 annas per rupee of the original land assessment. Rakta-manya-jamabandi seems to be the quit-rent collected from blood-grants, that is grants made to successors of the individuals who died fighting for the country or people. The terms Balutedars and Mohtarfa were used although there were Kannada equivalents, *viz., Ayagara* and *Angadi-patti*. On the other hand there are some Kannada terms which have lingered on even under Maratha administration. Such were *Komarki, Talavarki, Korpati, Ganacharki, Panchakarak, Gudi-pati, Lagna-karak* and *kamat-sardesai.* Komarki is obviously a tax on the blacksmith or *Kammaras*. Talavara was the village watchman, and *talavarki* might mean a tax collected for the Talara. *Kor* is batai, and *Korpati* might mean a tax collected from the ryots when the batai was made. *Ganacharki* was a tax levied on the Lingayat priests. Gudipati might be a tax either levied on the temples or for the temples. *Lagankarka* was a tax on marriages. *Kamat* signifies cultivation of land with one or more pairs of bullocks with necessary equipment. Kamat lands usually belonged to public servants or influential men, cultivated either by hired or compulsory labour. They did not let out these lands to others, but kept them for their own use.

1. KJ: 325

Nargund-Ramdurg Principality

Broadly speaking, there are three phases in the history of this principality. The first phase covers all the events leading to the foundation of the principality. The second phase, which could again be divided into several sub-phases, runs from 1705 when the principality was founded to 1810 when it was partitioned into two parts. The sub-phases are (i) 1705-1744, the Bhave rule before the first interregnum, (ii) the first interregnum, 1744-1760, when the Samsthan was under Balavant Appaji Suru, with small shares in the hands of Yogirao and Bhaskarrao; (iii) 1760-1785 from the first restoration to the second interregnum; (iv) the second interregnum, 1786-1792 when it was under the Peshwa rule; (v) 1792-1910 from the second restoration to the partition

The third phase covers the period of two separate principalities, the Nargund branch coming to an end in 1858, and the Ramdurg branch in 1948.

Shivaji is said to have built the forts of Nargund and Ramdurg about A.D. 1676, and appointed Ramachandra Pant Amatya in charge of the former. Ramachandra Pant entrusted its administration to one Appaji Suru. It was, however, captured by Aurangzeb in 1692, but was reconquered by Appaji Suru and his able co-adjutor Ramarao Dadajirao of Vetoshi in 1705. From that year onwards Ramarao, among other claimants, mainly began to rule from Nargund. It appears that the rulers of Nargund, though practically independent, never became totally free from the hegemony of either the Chhatrapatis of Kolhapur, or Ramchandra Pant Amatya or the Peshwa. An Ajnapatra of Shivaji II (Shahu) of Kolhapur dated 2-8-1714 says that the saranjam, the mukasa villages and the military contingents in the forts of Nargund, Navalgund and Ramdurg were continued to Ramachandra Pant Amatya as before.[1] Hence in the beginning Ramrao Dadaji seems to have been working under Ramchandra Pant Amatya to whom Nargund and Ramdurg were granted.

Genealogy of Nargund — Ramdurg Bhaves

(*based on the Bhave Kula-vrittanta, Pune, 1940*)

The same family of Bhaves ruled from two places, Nargund and Ramdurg. Hence we find many times the members of both the branches possessing the villages or enjoying the sanads together.

1. *Kokanachya Itihasachi Sadhane* (1692-1828) (Bombay, 1971): 7, p. 7.

Dadambhatta (Dadaji)I

- *Nargund Branch*
  - Balavantarao
    - Dadajirao II (1740-42)
    - Bhaskararao I (1760-73)
      - Vyentatarao (1773-85)
        - Dadajirao III (1817-42)
          - Bhaskararao II (1842-58)
- *Ramdurg Branch*
  - Ramarao I
    - Achyutarac
    - Yogirao I (1742-77)
      - Govindarao
        - Ramarao II (1777-85)
          - Narayanarao[1] (1810-27)
            - Ramarao III (1857-72)
              - Yogirao II (1872-77)
                - Vyenkatarao (1877-1907)
                  - Ramarao IV (1907-1949)

In 1711 Shahu granted in *inam* the village of Vetoshi to Ramrao. In the same year the Nawab of Savanur gave to Ramrao the Tarf of Konnur in *inam*, as Ramrao had helped him in some work.

Ramrao also got from many Sardars inam villages in return for the help rendered to them. Thus he got:

1. 6 inam villages like Asuti Karmadi, etc. from the jalihal Desai.
2. 3 villages like Hunasikatti from the Navalgund Desai.
3. Kaujagiri from the Dambal Desai.
4. Avaradi from the Huli Killedar.
5. 10 villages from the Torgal Desai.

1. After him, his wife ruled from 1829 to 1857.

6. Hattarvad from the Kittur Desai.
7. The inam village of jadara-hebli from the Nawab of Savanur.[1]

In 1715 Ramrao started levying the *Mokas-bab* and *Gadapatti* from the territory lying between the Ghataprabha and Tungabhadra, the dues which went to the Karavir Government earlier.

In 1734 Sambhaji II of Kolhapur granted to Dadajirao Bhaskar of Nargund the right to collect the Mokas-bab and Gadapatti in the above area

In 1719 the Chhatrapati of Kolhapur conferred the title of "*Sachiv*" and "*Samsthanik*" on Ramrao, granting him at the same time two inam villages of Mangevadi and Gangapur.

After Ramrao, Dadajirao himself was carrying on the administration of the state. Of the two wives of Ramrao, Lakshmibai was ambitious. In 1742 she got Dadajirao murdered. After the murder of Dadajirao, Ramrao's son Yogirao, probably by the second wife Gopikabai, became the ruler. He, with the support of the Council members, imprisoned Lakshmibai at Kittur. During the rule of Yogirao, the Havaldar of Nargund Banaji Ranasing and Appaji Suru's adopted son Balavantrao attempted to remove Yogirao from power.

In 1744 the Nargund Samsthan was divided into 3 parts: (1) one part was given to Yogirao, consisting of Ramdurg and 11 villages, all together rated at 38,000 rupees; (2) the second consisting of Idagal and other villages rated at 12,000 rupees to Bhaskarrao; and (3) the third comprising Nargund and other villages to Balavantrao. Really speaking, the Samsthan of Nargund was made over to Balavantrao, the Bhave brothers getting only small shares.

As a reward for helping Nana Saheb against the Nawab of Savanur in 1756, Ramrao was allowed to take Nargund from Balavantrao, which he did in 1760 with the help of Bhaskarrao and Lingoji Havaldar of the Ramdurg fort. The Peshwa granted to Balavantrao the Hebli village rated at 12,000 in lieu of the *mokas-bab* of Nargund.

In 1762 the Peshwa granted to Yogirao and Bhaskarrao jointly the *saranjam* of Nargund. In 1773 Raghunath Rao renewed the grant of Nargund and Ramdurg jointly to Yogirao and Vyenkatrao.

In 1785 Tipu captured Nargund and carried off Vyenkatrao, Kalopant Pethe, and Kalopant's married daughter. Ramrao of Ramdurg fled to Kankanavadi which was under the Patwardhans. After the Treaty of Gajendragad of 1787 Vyenkatrao of Nargund was released by Tipu.

1. Edward West, *MSMC*, pp. 173 ff.

In 1792 Sawayi Madhavrao regranted Nargund and Ramdurg principalities again jointly to Ramrao and Vyenkatrao.

After the death of Ramrao in 1800 his minor son Narayanrao became the ruler, his uncle Bapurao Ranade acting as the regent. In 1809 Bajirao II partitioned the Nargund-Ramdurg principality between Narayanrao of Ramdurg and Vyenkatrao of Nargund. Narayanrao got 41 villages rated at 87,355 rupees, while Vyenkatrao got 33 villages rated at 71,644 rupees. The Ramdurgkar also got the following 17 villages from the Nargundkar[1]:

1. Menasigi	2. Hebbal	3. Asoti
4. Somanakatti	5. Hadli	6. Jalikatti
7. Kittur	8. Kallapur	9. Sureban
10. Gonnagar	11. Huligoppa	12. Hosageri
13. Kitali	14. Chikkoppa	15. Avaradi
16. Sangal	17. Kalahal[2]	

In return the Ramdurgkar was to maintain a contingent of 113 troops and the Nargundkar of 112 troops for the service of the Peshwa.[3]

Narayanrao died in 1727. Owing to disputes about adoption, the Ramdurg State was under the administration of the Company from 1827 to 1829. But from 1829 to 1857 Radhabai, the widow of Narayanrao, ruled ably.

In 1872 after the death of Ramrao (1857—72), his minor adopted son Yogirao became the ruler, with Datye as his Karbhari. On the death of Yogirao in 1877, during the minority of his son Vyenkatrao (*i.e.*, from 1877 to 1900) the administration was carried on by a joint council of two Karbharis, one appointed by the Company, the other by the Ramdurgkar. The Company's nominee was Madhav Vishnu Masurkar. He fixed a reasonable land assessment and devised better methods for its collection.

After the death of Vyenkatrao in 1907, the Ramdurg administration was again under the Company during the minority of his son Ramrao from 1907 to 1915. During his rule only Ramdurg was finally merged with the Indian Union.

---

1. Ajnapatra of Bajirao Raghunath dated A.D. 1809 found in the Ramdurg Palace.
2. See also KJ: 240 Letter in Modi by Narayanarao Ram to Baba Saheb dated C. 1811 A.D.
3. In 1820 an agreement was signed between the Company and Narayanarao who accepted the Company's suzerainty

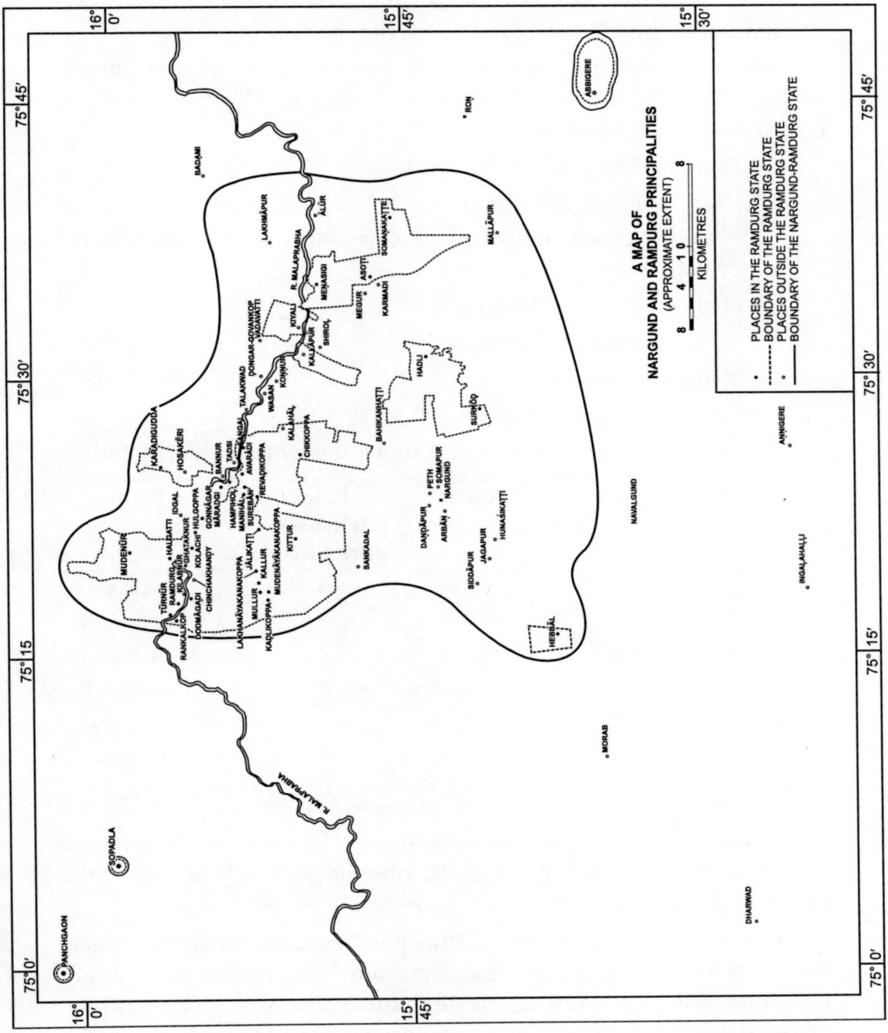
A MAP OF
NARGUND AND RAMDURG PRINCIPALITIES
(APPROXIMATE EXTENT)
KILOMETRES
PLACES IN THE RAMDURG STATE
BOUNDARY OF THE RAMDURG STATE
PLACES OUTSIDE THE RAMDURG STATE
BOUNDARY OF THE NARGUND-RAMDURG STATE
R. MALAPRABHA
BADAMI
RON
ABBIGERE
NAVALGUND
ANNIGERE
INGALAHALLI
MORAB
DHARWAD
SOPADLA
PANCHGAON
NARGUND
RAMDURG
HEBBAL
MUDENUR
KARADIGUDDA
HOSAKERI
LAKHMAPUR
ALUR
SOMANAKATTE
MALLAPUR
SURKOD
HADLI
BAHIKANHATTI
SANKADAL
KITTUR
SIDDAPUR
JAGAPUR
HUNASIKATTI
DANDAPUR
ARBAN
PETH
SOMAPUR
KONNUR
WASAN
TALAKWAD
SHIROL
KALLAPUR
KIYALI
MEGUR
KARMADI
ASOTI
MENASIGI
CHIKKOPPA
KALAHAL
REVADIKOPPA
AVARADI
SUREBAN
HAMPIHOL
MANIHAL
JALIKATTI
MUDENAYAKANAKOPPA
KALLUR
MULLUR
KADLIKOPPA
LAGHANAYAKANAKOPPA
CHINCHAKHANDY
DODMAGADI
RANIKALKOP
TURNUR
KILABNUR
GHATAKNUR
KOLACHI
HULGOPPA
HALBATTI
IDGAL
GONNAGAR
MARADGI
BANNUR
TADSI
16° 0'
15° 45'
15° 30'
75° 0'
75° 15'
75° 30'
75° 45'

Extent of the principality and the revenue it yielded:

In 1762, according to an Yadi Ajmas of Samsthan Nargund,[1] Madhavrao I made a grant of the Nargund Samsthan jointly to. Yogirao Ramrao (1742-77) and Bhaskarrao Dadaji (1760-73) as per the *beheda* of 1759.

The total yearly income or revenue from the Samsthan, according to this grant, was Rs. 2,47,251-3-0-3 (about 2½ lakhs). This revenue was to be collected under seven heads:

1. Pargana Nargund (23 villages).
2. Tarf Konnur (22 villages).
3. Pargana Navalgund, Pargana Govankop, Karyat Saudatti (12 villages).
4. Pargana Badami (6 villages).
5. Kille Ramdurg (12 villages).
6. Futgaon (4 villages).
7. Mokasbab and Gadapatti.

The revenue sums to be collected under these heads were as under:

	Rupees	Annas	Paise (Quarter anna pieces)	From
1.	58,414	14	3	(23 villages)
2.	33,812	3	3	(22 villages)
3.	19,848	4	2	(12 villages)
4.	23,240	10	0	(6 villages)
5.	16,326	7	3	(12 villages)
6.	22,437	8	0	(4 villages)
7.	73,171	12	0	(8 groups)
	2,47,251	12	3	

(1) In the Nargund Pargana the revenue was collected from the following 23 villages:

Qasba Nargund, Mauje Dandapur, Mauje Somapur, Mauje Peth, Mauje Arban, Majare Bahikanahatti, Majare Jagapur, Majare Karavinakop, Mauje Siddapur, Mauje Kittur, Mauje Alur, Mauje Gulkate, Mauje Hebli, Qasba Shirol, Mauje Wadawatti, Mauje Igalgundi, Qasba Hosakere, Mauje Hanamapur, Mauje Mastikate, Mauje Joginahal, Mauje Karadigudda, Mauje Karlakoppa, Mauje Kaulagikere.

---

1. KJ: 240: Yadi Ajmas Samsthan Nargund.

Shirol, Wadawatti and Igalgundi were from Samat Shirol and Hoskere, Hanampur, Mastikate, Joginahal, Karadigudda and Karlakoppa were from Samat Hosakere.

(2) In the Konnur Tarf the revenue was collected from the following 22 villages:

Qasba Konnur, Mauje Chikop, Mauje Kalahal, Mauje Soriban, together with the garden, Mauje Hulgop, Mauje Idgal, Mauje Aralikate, Mauje Maradgi, Mauje Lakhmapur, Mauje Biknur, Mauje Dongar Govanakop, Mauje Anagundi, Mauje Manihal, Mauje Gonnagar, Mauje Chikmulangi, Mauje Bennur, Mauje Tadsi, Mauje Sangal, Mauje Talakwad. Mauje Wasan, Mauje Mallapur, Mauje Hotiholiwas. Besides revenue was realized from Khedikop of Sardeshpande and Hagnur Inamgaon of Sardesai.

(3) In this group 12 revenue-paying villages were scattered among Pargana Navalgund, Pargana Govanakop and Karyat Saudatti as under:

Four villages from Tarf Mullur, Mauje Kadlikop, Mauje Jalikate, Mauje Lakhinayakanakop, Mauje Sankadal, Mauje Surkod, Mauje Hebbal, Mauje Hunasikatti. Qasba Govanakop.

(4) In Pargana Badami 6 villages were paying revenue: Mauje Menasigi, Mauje Kitali, Mauje Asoti, Mauje Megur, Karmadi, Mauje Somanakatte.

(5) In Kille Ramdurg revenue was realized from 12 villages: Qasba Turnur, Mauje Ghatakanur, Mauje Kilabanur, Mauje Chinchkhadi, Mauje Doddamagadi, Mauje Halgatti, Mauje Kolchi, Mauje Rankalakop, Mauje Sopada, Mauje Panchgaon, Mauje Mudenur, Kille Ramdurg Peth.

(6) Four stray villages paid the revenue under the head Futgaon: Aurawadi (Karyat Huli), Hatarwad, Qasba Hebli, Kavalur (Tarf Koppal).

(7) The *mokas-bab* and *gadapatti-bab*[1] were collected, according to the beheda, from different villages widely scattered as shown below:

(a) From Sarkar Savanur

- (1) Qasba Annigeri
- (2) Zakat Morab
  - (i) Pargana Guttal
  - (ii) Prant Ron

1. The *mokasa* and *gadapatti* are called *bab* here. The terms '*mukas-bab*' and '*gadapatti*' are used here, like '*nadgaudki*' and '*sahotra*' as definite dues which could be granted to anybody either for the services rendered by him to the state or as *inam*. Here the recipient was formerly the Chhatrapati of Kolhapur, and then the thief of Nargund-Ramdurg principality.

(b) Chik-Tadasi

(c) From Pargana Navalgund
Deshpande's Inamgaon Nagnur, Deskat etc.

(d) From Pargana Dharwad Qasba Dharwad, including garden and zakat dues

(e) Mauje Dhumwad

(f) From Zakat of
    (i) Betgeri
    (ii) Khanapur
    (iii) Dhumwad

(g) From Pargana Gadag
    (i) Mauje Umachgi
    (ii) Pargana Hubli
    (iii) Tarf Kittur
    (iv) Mauje Kowalwad
    (v) Mauje Alur (Pargana Kerur)
    (vi) Chavdi (Pargana Badami)
    (vii) Mauje Golarhal
    (viii) Mauje Inchinahal
    (ix) Mauje Kalapur
    (x) Mauje Baturki (Batkurki ?)
    (xi) Mauje Abbigeri.

(h) From Saranjami villages of the Patwardhans:
    (i) Pargana Lakshmeshwar
    (ii) Mauje Shekhad
    (iii) Pargana Rayara-Hubli
    (iv) Pargana Mulgund
    (v) Mauje Karlawad
    (vi) Qasba Igalahalli

Thus the sources of revenue were, broadly speaking, land revenue from the *Chali* lands, the *mokas-bab* and *gadapatti*, the *inam* villages given by various chiefs such as the Nawabs of Savanur, the Deshpande of Nagnur, the Desai of Gadag, the Saranjams of the Patwardhans, the Zakat dues, deskat dues, dues from garden lands and the like.

Some other revenue details are given in the *Nemnuk* of A.D. 1762 found in the Ramdurg Palace. The *Nemnuk* of Samsthan Nargund was granted (by Madhavrao Peshwa 1) according to the *beheda* of 1759 to Yogirao Ram and Bhaskarrao Dadaji jointly in 1762.

The Samsthan was rated at Rs. 2,47,251-3-0-3 This revenue was made up of three large sums as shown below:

I. the Saranjam rated at Rs. 2,06,832-1-1-0 enjoyed by Balavantrao (son of Appaji Suru).

II. Saranjam rated at Rs. 28,419-1-3-3 enjoyed by Yogirao.

III. Saranjam of Rs. 12,000-0-0-0 enjoyed by Bhaskarrao.

All these three saranjams had been given earlier as per the *beheda*. Now Balavantrao was deprived of his saranjam, which was given to Yogirao and Bhaskarrao in addition to their own saranjams. (A) The saranjam of Balavantrao was made up of the grant from the Govt. taluka, and the revenues from Venkatrao Narayan (Ichalkaranjikar), Govind Hari, Parasharam Ramchandra, Malharrao Bhikaji Raste.

(1) The revenue paid by Venkatrao Narayan came from (a) Navalgund Pargana (villages of Hunashikatte, Govankop, Hebbal, Jalikatte and Lakhanayakanakop of Karyat Saudatti and Sankadhal); (b) Mukas-bab from Pargana Nargund (the villages of Mugnur, Amargol, Aharhatti, Gadpatti, Alagasu, Gadasagar, Trimalapur, Haralikatte, Nayakanur). (c) Tarf Govanakop (villages of Banahatti, Banakanakop, Arasinagou, Khanapur, Madgunaki, Kusugal, Javur, Beganur), (d) Tarf Huli (villages of Adanur, Kapali), (e) Kamat of Ghanakavad and Nagarahali.

Some extra revenue was also received, though not included in the *beheda*. Such was from the share of the *inam* land of Navalgund Desai Jayagauda, Devara-gud-patti, Govanakop kamata, zakat from some villages of Pargana Navalagund, zakat from Qasba Dharwad, Uppina Betageri, Dhumwad in Pargana Mishrikot; Mokas-bab from Tarf Gadag as per *beheda*, from the inam village of Dambal Desai outside *beheda*.

(2) Govind Hari's revenue came from Parganas of Lakshmeshwar, Rayara Hubli and Kittur.

(3) Parashram Ramchandra's revenue came from Pargarta Mulgund.

(4) Malharrao Bhikaji Raste's dues were received from Parganas of Kerur and Badami.

(B) Similarly Yogirao's saranjam consisted of dues from Tarf Navalgund (villages of Surkod), from Govankop, Kavalur, Mullur, Jogarakop, Mudenayakanakop, One-third of *hak* of Jayagauda Desai Navalgundkar, *Zakat* from Konnur, *Mokas-bab* from Venkatrao Narayan's villages in Navalgund Pargana (villages of Balavatgi, Kongwad, Balehar, Khalagnur, Kallapur etc), Pargana Gadag, Kusugal, Khedikop the inam village of Mallappa Deshkulkarni of Mamle Torgal, Mauje Umachgi, the inam village (in Pargana Gadag) of Giridharrao Savanur, from Govind Hari's lands in Pargana Rayara Hubli, from Qasba Ingalahalli in Sarkar Torgal (Parashram Ramchandra), Mauje Kolwad in Pargana Govanakop (Savanurkar Mughal), Mauje Abbigere in Pargana Badami (Malhar Bhikaji Raste), Pargana Lokapur (Vyenkoji Ghorpade Mudholkar's mokas-bab).

(C) Bhaskarrao Dadaji's saranjam consisted of dues from Mauje Nagnur in Pargana Navalgund (the *mokas-bab* from the inam village of Girmaji Rakhmaji Deshkulkarni, Mauje Kitali in Pargana Badami (Malharrao Bhikaji) and from Pargana Konnur in the following villages: Sangal (Inam), Idagal, Baragur, Anagundi, Chikmulangi, Kalhal, Hagnur, Chikop.

Thus in the whole Samsthan the revenues received from—

1. Venkatarao Narayan were from—
   - (A) Pargana Navalgund
     - (a) the whole villages
     - (b) Mokas-bab
     - (c) dues from inam villages
     - (d) from the inam village of Nagnur Deshkulkarni
   - (B) Tarf Dharwad
   - (C) Pargana Gadag
     - (a) Mokas-bab
     - (b) Inam-gaon
   - (D) Tarf Koppal, from Kavalur lands.
2. Those received from Govind Hari were in—
   - (A) Pargana Lakshmeshwar
   - (B) Pargana Rayara Hubli
   - (C) Pargana Kittur.
3. Those from Parashram Ramchandra were in—
   - (A) Pargana Mulgund
   - (B) Sarkar Torgal
4. Those from Tofkhana in—

   Pargana Batkurki
5. Those from Malharrao Bhikaji Raste in—

(A) Pargana Kerur

(B) Pargana Badami

6. Those from Shinde Manolikar in—
   Mauje Goranhal Basidoni
7. Those from Savanurkar Mughal consisted of Gadapatti in—
   (A) Pargana Morab
   (B) Pargana Govankop
8. Those from Maloji Ghorpade consisted of Mokas-bab in—
   Karyat Lokapur
9. Those already enjoyed by Yogirao Ram and Bhaskarrao Dadaji were in—
   (A) Pargana Nargund
   (B) Pargana Badami.

Out of Rs. 2,47,251-12-3 a sum of Rs. 19000 was to be deducted for maintaining the contingent of 350 Swars, 300 by Balavantrao and 50 by Yogirao Ram, and thus a balance of Rs. 2,28,251-12-3 only was to be given to Yogirao Ram and Bhaskarrao Dadaji as per this *Nemnuk*. Although these revenues were assigned to the Bhaves by Madhavrao I, in some cases the Bhaves found it difficult to realise the revenue, especially from the Sardars of the Peshwa. Hence in 1769 Madhavrao I exhorted the concerned Sardars regarding the payment of mukasa and other dues to the Bhaves of Nargund, and also to the Vyenkatesh temple at Nargund.[1]

The letters were addressed to

1. Anandrao Bhikaji regarding the payment to the god Vyenkatesh of Nargund, of dues from Qasba Ron, Jalihal and Badami.
2. Vira-Mallappa Desai of Kittur regarding the payment of mukasa of Rs. 1300 from the Inamgaon Hatarwad in Pargana Kittur.
3. Khanderao Goso of Savanur for payment of dues of Rs. 950 from five villages, *viz.* Qasba Annigeri, Mauje Hanchinahal, Zakat Morab, Pargana Guttal and Mauje Kavalvad, in Taluka Savanur.
4. Narayanrao Ballal regarding the payment to the Vyenkatesh temple of Nargund Rs 262½, being the dues from Mauje Kekhad in Pargana Gadag, Alangvad in Pargana Navalgund (5 *mars* of land), Mauje Javur in Pargana Navalgund.

1. Pune Archives, Ghadni/Beheda: 453.

5. Bapuji Suryavamshi Dinkar for payment of dues from some lands in Mauje Kadadhali of Pargana Navalgund.
6. Krishnaji Madhavrao regarding payment of *mukas-bab* of Rs.1000 from Pargana Batakurki.

The principality under the administration of the Peshwa

From 1786 to 1792 the Nargund principality was directly under the Peshwa. In 1788 it was administered by a Maratha officer named Raghunath Chintaman. At this time the administrative divisions and the villages they contained were as under:[1]

	Total		Villages alienated		Amali
1. Pargana Nargund	32	--	10	=	22
2. Tarf Konnur	29	--	10	=	19
3. Samat Badami	6	--	1	=	5
4. Tarf Navalgund	10	--	7	=	3
	77		28		49

The total income of this year including the arrears of the previous year was Rs. 1,81,797-2-1-2.

From a Terij[2] of the same year (A.D. 1788) of the Nargund Taluka with the same Maratha officer incharge, *viz.* Raghunath Chintaman, we know the following details :

	Adm. Divn.	No. of villages	Revenue
	Pargana Nargund	13	
1.	Samat Sirol	3	8628-15-0
	Samat Hoskeri	6	
2.	Tarf Konnur	19	5644-10-1
3.	Tarf Navalgund	3	1115-10-0
4.	Pargana Badami	5	3101-14-0
		49	18491-1-1

Alienated villages in the Samsthan:

From an important document in the Pune Archives,[3] we get the details of the alienated lands in the Nargund principality just one year before the partition between Nargundkar and Ramdurgkar.

1. KJ: 240. More details of Taluka under the officer Raghunath Chintaman are given in the sequel.
2. KJ: 240 : Terij.
3. KJ: 240 : Zamin-zada Inamat, dated A.D. 1808.

	Village	Alienated lands in *mars*
(A) (1)	Qasba Nargund	10
(2)	Qasba Dandapur	13
(3)	Mauje Somapur	28
(4)	Mauje Peth	7
(5)	Mauje Arban	4-2-0
(6)	Mauje Gulkate	6
(7)	Majare Jagapur	6
(8)	Majare Bhairanahatti	7
(9)	Majare Karavinakop	3
(10)	Mauje Siddapur	3
(11)	Mauje Chik-Nargund	9
(12)	Mauje Hadli	40
(13)	Samat Sirval	8
(14)	Mauje Kalkere	5-2-0
(15)	Mauje Kittur	15
(16)	Mauje Hanasikate	11
(17)	Mauje Jalikati	1
(18)	Mauje Lakinayakanakop	3
(19)	Mauje Sankadahal	7
		187-3-0
Less:	because of damage due to survey, etc.	19-0-2
Balance		168-2-2
		Mars of Land

These lands were assigned for different purposes as shown below

(B) (1)	Devadaya	: 14-1-0
(2)	Bramhadaya	: 67-0-0
(3)	Mathamanya	: 5-2-0
(4)	Hospitality	: 2-2-0
(5)	Sarkar Nargund Puratan	: 17-0-0
(6)	Kalopant Pethe	: 5-0-0
(7)	Inamdar Puratan	: 17-0-0
(8)	Mahadaji Pant Behedekar	: 2-0-0
(9)	Chakar-manya	: 4-0-0
(10)	Waste land	: 6-2-0
(11)	Jamindar of Sankadahal (unaccounted, unlawfully enjoyed)	: 7-0-0

A Zamin-Zada[1] again found in the Pune Archives throws interesting light on the alienated lands described as *Inamat* and *Sardeshkat* in Pargana Nargund and Tarf Konnur measured in terms of *mars*.The lands were known as *rayarekhe* lands.

In Pargana Nargund there were 187-3-0 *mars* of such lands in 19 villages.

In Tarf Konnur there were 87-0-0 *mars* of alienated lands in 25 villages.

Thus in 44 villages there were in all 274-3-0 *mars* of land.

From 182-3-2 *mars* were deducted owing to various reasons as shown below:

(1)	Owing to damage, etc.	19-0-2
(2)	Sarvamanya with temples	19-1-0
(3)	Dharmadav with Brahmins	84-0-0
(4)	Baje Inamdar	24-0-0
(5)	Sardesai's nemnuk	5-0-0
(6)	Mathamanya	6-0-0
(7)	Vahivat with Ramdurgkar	24-0-0
(8)	Hospitality of Fakirs	2-2-0
		182-3-2

In connection with No. 2 above, we get references to the previous rulers of Nargund. It or some portions of it were successively under the rule of Desai, Tipu, Trimbakrao Anna, Bhanu, Sivarao Desai and Rao Saheb.

From 1786 to 1792 the administration of Nargund was directly under the Peshwa Government. Nargund was turned into a taluka consisting of several villages grouped under different administrative divisions.

We know from a taleband found in the Pune Archives that in 1787-88 the taluka of Nargund was in charge of a Maratha officer named Raghunath Chintaman.

The sources of income were (1) the land revenue which constituted a major portion, (2) extra revenue called *sivaye*, (3) the *kamavis*, (4) *izafat* (an appropriation of revenue by the Sarsubadars in the southern provinces in addition to the revenue they were to pay to the State — Wilson), (5) granary contributions, and (6) loans.

The total revenue of taluka Nargund for 1787-88 was Rs. 1,81,797-9-6 (nearly two lakhs). Its break-up was as follows:

---

1. KJ: 240, dated A.D. 1817.

Rs.	6,208-3-0	Net revenue realized village-wise.
Rs.	10,286-8-0	*Sivaye* collection
Rs.	10,096-9-6	*Kamavis*
Rs.	50,000-0-0	*Izafat*
Rs.	44-9-6	Granary dues
Rs.	44,955-8-9	Loans
Rs.	180,490-8-9	
+ Rs.	1,307-2-9	previous year's arrears
Rs.	181,797-9-6	Total

The net revenue included the amounts realized from (1) 22 villages of Pargana Nargund, (2) 19 villages of Tarf Konnur (3) 5 villages of Samat Badami and (4) 3 villages of Tarf Navalgund. It may thus be noted that taluka Nargund consisted of 1 pargana, 1 samat, and 2 tarfs. The Pargana was the biggest administrative division in the taluka, and consisted of 32 villages. Next came the Tarf. Tarf Konnur was composed of 29 villages while Tarf Navalgund had only 10 villages. The Samat was the smallest administrative division consisting of 6 villages only.

Although there were in all 91 villages in these four administrative divisions of taluka Nargund, 42 were in private hands such as Inamdars and Desais, while only 49 were taxable by the Government. These were termed *amali* lands and are comparable to the *Khalsa* lands under Mughals.

The private land-owners or Zamindars included (1) Navalgundkar Desai (2) Badri Zamal Khan, (3) Nargund Deshpande, (4) Hosakere Desai, (5) Shirol Desai (6) Venkatrao Bhaskar in Tarf Konnur, (7) Ramadurgkar, (8) Deshpande Torgalkar, (9) Narasimha Dikshit Karigovinakoppa, and (10) Ramarao Govind.

The *Sivaya* income appears to have been made up of quit-rent from some Inamdars, perquisites unclaimed, the fees levied while Inams changed hands, and the produce from the government mango groves and gardens, especially when the right to enjoy them lapsed to the government from the grantees.

The *Kamavis* was constituted by the sums paid by the highest bidders to the state for having received the contract or monopoly of the right to collect the revenue and also to run the markets in some specific villages, by the presents of money made by nobles, and by judicial dues.

We can thus roughly note that (1) revenue (including *Kamavis*) from the various villages was about 821½ thousand, the *Izafat* 50 thousand, the granary dues about 45 only, the loan about 48 thousand, and the total about 2 lakhs.

The items of expenditure were (1) the salaries to the Government servants (*Karkuns*) in the civil services, (2) salaries to the royal army-Gardis and Rohilas, (3) salaries to the *Shibandi Hasham* and *Baje Hasham*, (4) temples and temple services, (5) *daftar kharch*, (6) *dasara kharch*, (7) *taivaj kharch* (the expenses incurred for furnishing betel leaves and nuts to guests and visitors), (8) celebration of festivals, (9) lighting lamps on the forts etc., (10) boarding charges, (11) discounts for cashing bills for exchange (hundanavali) and interest paid on loans, (12) building and repairing expenses, (13) expenses for military planning (*masalat kharch*), (14) expenses for sending reinforcements (*kumaki kharch*), and (15) liquidation of debts. This gives us a glimpse into the administration of Taluka Nargund under the Peshwas.

APPENDIX A

Administration of Southern Maratha Country in the pre-Maratha or Adilshahi period

In the heyday of its power the Bijapur kingdom is said to have consisted of the following 12 Subas, namely: Bijapur, Belgaum, Solapur, Raichur, Miraj, Bankapur, Naldurg, Bidar, Gulbarga, Bangalore, Madura and Tanjore[1]. However, the area that was directly under the Adilshahi administration seems to have been much smaller, Subas such as Bangalore, Madura and Tanjore being largely ruled by the feudatory chiefs of the Adilshahs.

After its conquest, the Mughals organised the Bijapur kingdom into 18 Sirkars, namely, Haveli Bijapur, Miraj, Azamnagar, Panhala, Raibag, Malikwad, Karnataka, Bankapur, Torgal, Gazipur, Adawani, Mudgal, Sagar, Raichur, Dabhol, Naldurg, Malkhed and Gulbarga.[2]

In Southern Maratha Country between the Krishna and Tungabhadra rivers there were three Sarkars in Suba Bijapur, namely: Azamnagar, Torgal and Bankapur. The exact extent of the Bijapur Suba is, however, not ascertainable at the present state of our knowledge. The earliest document[3] available in the Peshwa Daftar relating to Torgal area is dated A.D. 1667 and speaks of Pargana Nargund in Mamle Torgal. In 1688 also Torgal was a Mamla. By 1699, however, Torgal had become a Sarkar in Suba Dar-ul-Jafar Bijapur[4]. At the same time Torgal was also known as

1. S.K. Sinha, *Medieval History of the Deccan*
2. KJ: 1938 : 694.
3. KJ: 241 : 354.
4. KJ: 241 : 357.

a Sarkar in 1686, along with Azamnagar and Bankapur Sarkars, when they were bestowed on the Nawab of Savanur by Aurangzeb on the fall of Bijapur. At this time there were 22 Mahals in Bankapur Sarkar, namely, Pargana, Kundgol, Pargana Karadgi-Kamatran, Pargana Mishrikot, Samat Kalghatgi, Samat Bamigatti, Samat Tadas, Samat Hirekerur, Samat Chikkerur, Samat Kod, Samat Kagineli, Pargana Ranebennur, Samat Nidsangi, Samat Shiggaon, Pargana Hangal, Pargana Bankapur, Pargana Tilavalli, Pargana Adur, Kupelur, Samat Masur, Peth-Qasba Haveri, Peth Hamsbavi and Dehat-Kille Airani.[1]

The Sarkars of Azamnagar and Torgal together contained the following 36 Mahals: Pargana Bagalkot-Bilagi, Pargana Azamnagar-Belglum-Shahapur, Qasba Tegur-Tadkod, Hisar Dharwad, Pargana Lakshmeshwar, Pargana Jalihal-Badami, Pargana Mulgund, Pargana Rayara Hubli, Hissar Harihar, Pargana Anawal, Pargana Yadwad, Pargana Murgod, Pargana Pachchhapur, Pargana Sampgaon-Kittur, Qasba Narendra, Hisar Babhal, Pargana Navalgund, Pargana Guttal, Qasba Annigeri, Qasba Devara Hubli, Sul Byahatti, Pargana Ghanadurg, Pargana Bannur, Pargana Sattigeri, Pargana Gokak, Taluka Betgeri, Qasba Aminbhavi, Qasba Yekkundi, Pargana Gadag, Pargana Rattihalli, Qasba Jadara Hebli, Rao Mugud, Pargana Kerur Salabat Khan, Pargana Likapur, Pargana Kadkol and Tarf Konnur.

A Modi document of 1680 mentions Bankapur and Azamnagar alias Bailgaon Sarkars of Subha Dar-ul-Jafar Bijyapur and gives a list of 16 villages each in Bankapur and Azamnagar. The villages in Sarkar Bankapur were Pargana Haveli Bankapur, Pargana Lakshmeshwar, Pargana Rayara Hubli, Pargana Masur, Pargana Gadag, Pargana Karadgi, Pargana Kamatran, Pargana Dharwad, Pargana Kundgol, Pargana Naregal, Pargana Mishrikot, Pargana Rattihalli, Pargana Hangal, Pargana Halyal, Pargana Harihar and Pargana Honnali.

Similarly the villages in Sarkar Azamnagar were Pargana Haveli from Bijapur, Pargana Lat, Pargana Solapur, Pargana Hubli, Pargana Hukkeri, Pargana Ajira, Pargana Gokak alias Rahmatgaon, Pargana Kabbur, Pargana Nesari, Pargana Padshapur, Pargana Khanapur alias Hosur, Pargana Hubli-Sampgaon, Pargana Kapshi, Pargana Sadalge, Pargana Munoli and Pargana Vitur.[2]

The power structure in Southern Maratha Country in the Krishna-Tungabhadra Doab depended on a variety of factors. The over-all rule of the Adilshah was felt especially through his Wazirs and nobles. Under

1. *Dilerjangi*, p. 18.
2. KJ: 270 : 170.

Ibrahim Adilshah, Mustafa Khan and Khawas Khan were very powerful nobles. First Mustafa Khan was the Wazir, but his position was usurped by Khawas Khan. The latter was, however, murdered in 1635. Thereafter Mustafa Khan again became the Wazir. Mustafa wielded great influence in higher circles, and even gave his daughter in marriage to Muhammad Adil Shah.[1] To this struggle between two nobles another element was added with the coming of Khan-i-Khanan Khan Muhammad (He was also known as Ikhlas Khan) who was earlier an Abyssinian slave. (*HS*, p. 93).

Khawas Khan, the second son of *Khan-i-Khanan* became the Wazir in 1672, but was soon to be replaced by another Khawas Khan who was in power from 1672 to 1675. Now yet another element, a noble from Afghanistan, namely, Abdul Karim Bahlol Khan, was added to the nobility. Abdul Karim Bahlol Khan who stepped in as Wazir in 1675 continued to hold that office till his death in 1677.

It may be noted that Khawas Khan, the son of Khan-i-Khanan, was the leader of the Deccani faction while Bahlol Khan was the leader of the Afghan faction. As noted above, during Sikandar Adilshah's reign the Bankapur Sarkar with 22 Mahals was granted to him in jagir. He also held Miraj as a jagir.[2] His father Abdul Rahim was enjoying Koppal as his jagir.

As Abdul Rahim's son Abdul Karim was a very influential noble, and also the Wazir, other nobles courted his friendship. They even established matrimonial relations with him. Masaud Khan, the chief of Adoni, gave his daughter in marriage to Abdul Karim. This won him the support of the Abyssinian group in the Bijapur court. He also got Bagalkot by way of dowry. As Masaud himself was the son-in-law of Siddi Jauhar, the latter also gave his support to Abdul Karim.[3]

Although the people in these three Sarkars or Mamle were vaguely under the sway of the Central Government of Bijapur or under some Wazir, they were immediately under the rule of the Bijapur bureaucracy at the Mamla and Pargana levels. Thus in a document of A.D. 1613 the officer representing the central government in Mamla Bankapur is addressing the lower officials, Mukaddams and raiyats of Qasba Haveri which was included in Mamla Bankapur.[4] Another document of 1685 gives us to understand that at this time Sharzakhan was the Adilshahi officer in the Gadag area.[5] Similarly by about 1626 Alafkhan was in

1. *Basatinussalatin*, 307-314, *Padisbabnama* of Abdul Hamud Lahori, 360, 404 in *House of Shivaji*, p. 93.
2. Sarkar, *HS*, p. 16.
3. E.W. West, *MSMC*, p. 206.
4. *SCS*: 6 : 13.
5. *SCS*: 6 : 24.

charge of Pargana Gadag.[1] From 1643 to 1679 Ikhlas Khan was the officer in charge of Koppal area.[2]

In a letter[3] dated 1643 the Desai of Killa Koppal was asked to obey the orders of the new Thanedar, and to see that the Mokasis in the (Koppal) Pargana would get their dues properly. A letter[4] of 1646 shows how a certain Viththal Suro in league with certain Adilshahi officers such as Fattekhan Qadiri murdered Banavarasa, the Desai of Koppal, and his son. When this was reported to Ikhlas Khan, he wrote this comforting letter to the brother of Banavarasa. Viththal Suro was the son of Suro Viththal, and this Viththal Suro, taking the help of Malik Sarnobat, had even seized forcibly some villages belonging to Banavarasa. Finally Janiyappa, heir to Banavarasa, could get back the office of Desai which rightly belonged to him.[5]

Letter Nos. 37, 38, 55 show how the Desai was ordered to see that the Mokasa dues were properly paid to the Mokasi of Sidogi named Khan Makdum Shah.[6]

In 1679 an *Abhayapatra* was sent to Remanna Desai of Koppal. The Karkun of the Koppal fort had plundered the villages of Remanna Desai. Frightened by the menace of this Karkun, Remanna had given up the duties of the Desai's office. He was now persuaded to take up his responsibility of Desai's office once again.[7] The officer who was exercising power over the workers of the Koppal fort was a Sardar called Abdul Qadir Mayana.

As in Gadag and Koppal, so in Lakeshmeshwar there was a Bijapuri bureaucratic officer exercising power over that Pargana. In 1622-23 a certain Mir Ali Raza was the Havaldar of Bankapur Mamla.[8] At this time Pargana Iakshmeshwar was included in Mamla Bankapur. In 1634 Ankushkhan bin Manjulkhan was the Shahi officer in charge of this area.

Generally in medieval times the people were governed and their activities regulated by four types of powers, namely, *Amatya-satta* or governmental power, *Deshakasatta* of the power of the hereditary officers, *Jnati-satta* or the power of the indigenous religious and social bodies, and *Vyapara-satta* or the power of commercial bodies. In the *Deshaka-satta*

1. *Ibid.*, 29.
2. *Ibid.*, 32-41.
3. *Ibid.*, 36.
4. *Ibid.*, 40.
5. *Ibid.*, 6 : 42.
6. *Ibid.*, 6 : 37, 38, 55.
7. *SCS*: 6 : 43.
8. *Ibid.*, 59.

the power exercised by the Watandars such as Desai, Deshmukh, Patil, etc is mainly included.

In Belgaum the rule of the Adilshahs began in the times of Ismail Adil Shah. As Asad Khan Lari, who was a Persian from the Province of Lar, assisted Ismail in his deliverance from his guardian, he conferred on him Belgaum as his jagir in 1511. (In 1519 Asad Khan completed the building of the Masjid Safa in the Belgaum fort. He also constructed the fort of Miraj.)

In 1535 we find Ain-ul-Mulk Gulani at Hukkeri, Asad Khan at Belgaum and Yusuf Turk in possession of the Kittur jagir. Under Ibrahim Adilshah, Asad Khan was created prime minister as well as commander-in-chief. Asad Khan died at Manoli in 1549 having held Belgaum for 38 years. Thereafter Mohammad Kishvar Khan, the son of Asad Khan, became governor of the districts of Hukkeri, Belgaum and Raibag.

It was in the Talikota battle that the ancestor of the Navalgund chief, now the Desai of Sirsangi (1570) in this area, first came prominently into notice. The founder of the family was called Vitta Gauda, and was the Patel of Avaradi on the Bhima. The Padshah rewarded him for his service by creating him *Sardesai* of Torgal Prant in A.D. 1566.

In 1573 Dharwad was taken from one of the officers of Rama Raya of Vijayanagara. Bankapur was taken shortly afterwards. Ranadulla Khan is said to have possessed Hukkeri from 1569 to 1615.

Amin Mustafa Khan Banda Muhammad Sultan[1] administering from Hubli in 1684, Yusuf Poladkhan[2] of Hubli in 1657-58, Khan Azam Aqsim Khursid Khan[3] of Bankapur fort in 1579-80, officers such as these manned the important offices at the district level. Some of them were district officers, and some others were the commandants of the forts. These constitued the upper rung of the ruling class in districts or Mamlas.

Next to this small class of Muslim bureaucrats we find a bigger class of local hereditary officers consisting mostly of Desais, Nadgaudas, Nadkarnis and also Sardesais. Some of them were even the chiefs of small fiefs called Desgats. Such were Narsingrao Desai[4] of Dharwad Desgat (1675), Hanamarao Deuji Desai[5] and Deshkulkarni of Pargana

1. *SCS* : 6 : 6.
2. *Ibid.*, 8.
3. LD : 264.
4. *SCS.*
5. *SCS* : 6 : 8.

Rayara Hubli (1657-58), Srinivas Venkatadri Jois of Gadag[1] (1661) who was also the Deshkulkarni and Nadgauda of Pargana Gadag, Pawadi Naik[2] who was the Desai of Jalihal (1671-1696), Uducha Nayak of Kanakagiri[3], Viranagauda Devanagauda (1579-80), Kenchangauda (1634), and Khangauda II, who were the Desais of Lakshmeshwar.[4] These Desais often got *farmans* from the Adilshah or his officer which conferred on them the Desgats or some watans by way of remuneration for their services. Thus the *Watan* of the Dharwad Desgat was continued by a *farman* of Sikandar Adilshah to Narsingrao Desai, the son of Vyasarao Desai who was the founder of the Desgat of Dharwad. To Srinivas Venkatadri Jois, who was the Desai, Deshkulkarni and the Nadgauda of Pargana Gadag, was granted in 1661 Mauje Harlapur along with *mahasul, betbegar, farmaisi, sayar, patibab, zakat,* etc.[5] In 1659 the Adilshah granted to Uducha Nayaka, the Desai of Kanakagiri, a *farman* conferring on him, as before, the *hisar* of Kanakagiri.[6] The commandant of the Bankapur fort, Khan Azam Qasim Khursid Khan, granted to Viranagauda, the Desai of Lakshmeshwar, the *gaudike* of Budihal[7] in 1579-80.

These hereditary officers whose position was recognised by the Adilshahs as chiefs of small desgats or fiefs often monopolised more than one office. The Lakshmeshwar Desais were not merely the Desais of Lakshmeshwar sime, but became the Desais of Kille Koppal sime and also the Nadgaudas of Rayara Hubli sime.[8] Similarly Srinivas Venkatadri Jois was not merely the Desai, but also the Deshkulkarni and the Nadgauda of Pargana Gadag.[9]

Next to the Desais, Deshkulkarnis and Nadgaudas, the mayors of towns and the commercial elements enjoyed considerable power and position in the villages, and finally came the village officials such as the Gaudas, Kulkarnis and Talwars who also exercised power in their local areas. They also enjoyed tax-free lands in return for their services. The pontiffs of the Sringeri Math, of the Satyabodh Math at Savanur, and also the temple priests in villages had their own share of tax-free

1. *Ibid.*, 20.
2. Kaifiyat.
3. *SCS* : 6 : 129.
4. LD : 74.
5. *SCS* : 6 : 20.
6. *Ibid* : 129.
7. LD : 264.
8. LD : 74.
9. *SCS* : 6 : 20.

lands and they could influence the masses in religious matters. All this is abundantly proved by a number of original unpublished Modi documents available in the Peshwa archives. In Pargana Nargund of Mamle Torgal in 1667 the Desais, Deshkulkarnis and Nadgaudas enjoyed 13 *mars* of sarvamanya lands and the Sringeri Pontiff had 6 *mars* of sarvamanya lands. Among the local magnates the Patel, Kulkarni, Pattanasetti, and Talwar were the Judi landholders. The Patel seems to have been very influential, holding as many as 30 *mars* of land as against the Kulkarni who held only 5 *mars* of land, the Pattanasetti who had only 2 *mars* and the Talawar who had 4 *mars* of land.[1]

APPENDIX B

Inams in Dharwad[2]

Dharwad has gone through many vicissitudes in history. In medieval times it was included in the Vijayanagara Empire. On the fall of Vijayanagara, it passed under the sway of Bijapur. It had a strong fort, and there was a separate commandant of the fort Since it lay on the highway from Miraj in the north to Bankapur in south, it occupied a strategic importance. Aurangzeb took possession of it after defeating Bijapur in 1686. Its name was changed into Nashirabad. It was under the Mughals until Nana Saheb Peshwa conquered it in 1753. Under the Peshwas it was considered to be the doorway to the south, and was on the road leading to Srirangapattana.

As Dharwad was regarded as an important place politically, strategically and also commercially, it gradually developed into a flourishing town. In the beginning there was only a fort, but in due course the areas round the fort began to be peopled, and across the tank called Halgere to the south there came into existence the nucleus of a town in the form of various market places set up along different lanes. Thus the Shukrawar Peth, the Mangalwar Peth, the Adityawar Peth or the Javali Peth sprang up. Round this town and the fort many villages and hamlets also began to develop and gain in importance. Such were, for example, Rayapur, Haveri Peth, Madihal, Saptapur, and Navalur. Many of these villages have now become the suburbs of the Dharwad town.

In the Pune Archives there are a number of *Kaifiyats* which throw light on the development of this town. They give us a glimpse into the economic, social and cultural conditions of Dharwad in medieval times.

1. KJ : 241 : 354.
2. Dharwad is the headquarters of a district of the same name in Karnataka.

They supply information regarding the different taxes levied at different times by different rulers, the religious sects prevailing in those days, various grants made to temples, mathas, watandars and other individuals either as *inam* or as *mokasa*.

Krishnacharya, son of Ramachandracharya, and grandson of Sheshacharya, surnamed Vyasasamudra was the priest of the Vyenkatesh temple at the Shukrawar Peth of Kasha Dharwad. He was in possession of a *bele* of land in Navalur granted as *inam* for the temple of the god Sri Vyenkatesh. The land was a dry land, and had no mango trees in it. Since the land was totally an *inam* land, no tax or imposition such as *judi*, *yekasali* or *najarana* was paid for it.

This land was granted originally to Krishnacharya's father Ramachandracharya in the times of Tipu Sultan. After the death of Ramachandracharya, his son Rangacharya who was elder than Krishnacharya, was in possession of the land, and after the death of Rangacharya the land went to Krishnacharya, during the Company's rule in India.

This land was cultivated by the ryots on the terms of *lavani*. Deducting the expenses of cultivation from the gross produce, the average annual income from the land was Rs. 21-8-0.

Besides the produce of the land, Krishnacharya was getting some other grants from the Government and some voluntary contributions from the people for the service of the god Vyenkatesh The sources of income were the following:

(1) Rs. 21-8-0	Average annual income from the inam land, as noted above.
(2) Rs. 87-9-0	Annual grant from the Government Treasury for celebrating the chariot festival of the god, for the daily food offerings to the god and for burning a perpetual lamp before the god.
(3) Rs. 3-8-0	Being the exchange value of one Dharwadi (gold) coin (or hon) from Desai Ramrao.
(4) Rs. 3-8-0	Being the exchange value of one Dharwadi (gold) coin from Jivanarao Deshpande.
(5) Rs. 3-8-0	Being the exchange value of one Dharwadi (gold) coin from the Nadgauda.
	Thus Rs. 10-8-0 were offered by the three Mahal Jamidars of Dharwad every year for the Chariot festival of the god.

Thus the total annual income for the services of the god Vyenkatesh was Rs. 119-9-0.

The yearly expenses were as follows:

(1)	Rs. 12-0-0	For the daily food offerings to the god at the rate of one rupee for month; annually twelve rupees.
(2)	Rs. 12-0-0	For the expenses of oil for burning two lamps perpetually before the god.
(3)	Rs. 4-0-0	For purchasing a pair of dhotees for the god every year at the price of four rupees.
(4)	Rs. 12-1-0	For the yearly expenses on repairs of the temple, on erecting the pandal on the occasion of the Navaratra celebrations, and on whitewashing the temple walls and ceilings.
(5)	Rs. 21-0-0	For feeding the Brahmins daily during the Navaratra festival and for the great community lunch generally at the end of the festival.
(6)	Rs. 5-0-0	For feeding the Brahmins and for their *dakshina*.
(7)	Rs. 2-0-0	For repairing the "vehicles of gods" during the festival, by way of wages to the Jinagars.
(8)	Rs. 10-0-0	During the Vehicle Festival at night the wages paid to the man at the rate of one rupee per day for ten days.
(9)	Rs. 8-0-0	To courtesans
(10)	Rs. 3-0-0	For playing the band
(11)	Rs. 1-0-0	To the Brahmin expounding the Puranas.
(12)	Rs. 4-0-0	For repairs of the chariot
(13)	Rs. 4-0-0	For expenses on oil during the Car Festival.
Total	Rs. 98-1-0	

Deducting the annual expenditure of Rs. 98-1-0 from the annual income of Rs. 119-9-0, the priest was left with a profit of Rs. 21-8-0. This was how permanent arrangements were made for conducting the various types of services in the Vyenkatesh temple at the Sukrawar Peth of Qasba Dharwad or Nashirabad.[1]

1. KJ: 1597.

Another *Kaifiyat* throws light on the office of Mulla in a suburb of Dharwad. This *Kaifiyat* gives the genealogy of the occupant of the office of Mulla in the village of Malapur,[1] included in the Mahal of Dharwad. In 1844 Mulla Mohi-ud-din, son of Bade-Miya and grandson of Raje Mahmad was the occupant of this office.

In Malapur the Mulla was enjoying a land of 6 beles[2] as *inam* Although this piece of land was granted as an *inam* originally, a quit-rent came to be levied on it, and hence it was turned into a *judi-inam* land. It was a dry land, containing no mango trees. The quit-rent or the *judi* began to be levied under the Peshwas while originally Aurangzeb had granted it to the original grantee as a complete *inam* land. The quit-rent for 6 *beles* or 12 *annas* (*i.e.*, 4 *annas* less for a *guntha*) of land was 87 rupees. Till A.D. 1825 (1234 Fasli) Bade-Miya, father of Mohi-ud-din was paying this quit-rent and after his death in that year his son began to pay it to the Government.

The original inam was granted by Aurangzeb in A.D. 1690 (1102 A.H.) to the ancestor of Mohi-ud-din named Shaikh Daud, son of Shaikh Raja. Mohi-ud-din belonged to the 14th generation of Shaikh Daud. The Kaifiyat says that at the close of the Peshwa rule about 131 years had elapsed since the grant of the original *inam* land to Shaikh Daud. This *inam* had never been attached till 1844 when this Kaifiyat was submitted. Mohi-ud-din had a hereditary right to the enjoyment of this *judi-inam* land. On the death of Bade-Miya, the land was automatically inherited by Mohi-ud-din, there being no necessity to take the permission of the Govt. for inheritance. He inherited the land during the Company's rule.

Unfortunately this *inam* land of 12 *annas* was reduced by about 3 *annas* owing to two reasons. Unexpectedly a stream changed its course and began to flow through this land Secondly a strip of land, probably on either side of the stream, began to be used as a path. Thus Mohi-ud-din really had only 9 *annas* of land.

Deducting the expenses of cultivation from the total yield of the land, Mohi-ud-din got only 100 rupees as the output from the land. This land was not cultivated actually by the inam-holder, but was given to a cultivator for cultivation on a rental basis. The cultivator was required to till this land, grow crops on it, take some stipulated part of the yield

1. At present Malapur is a suburb of the town of Dharwad.
2. A *bele* was a denomination of the Vijayanagar coin *Varaha*. A *Varaha* contained 10 *hanas*, and the *hana* 8 *beles* or 16 *visas*. In land measurements the *hana* was equated with a *guntha* and its sixteenth part (*visa*) was called an *anna*. Thus a *guntha* consisted of 16 *annas* or 8 *beles* of land.

for himself and the remaining which was worth Rs. 100, was to be surrendered to the inam-holer. Out of this sum of Rs. 100, Rs. 87 were paid, as noted above, as judi or quit-rent to the Govt. and thus only Rs. 13 constituted the net yield of the land for Mohi-ud-din.

The various sources of income for this office, besides the above inam-land, and the expenses incurred on account of this office, and the balance that ultimately went to Mohi-ud-din were as follows:

(A) Other Sources of income:

Rs.	13	The net yield from his inam-land, as shown above.
Rs.	2	On account of Moharram, which the Govt. sent to the office in Taluka Dharwad every year
Rs.	3	On account of the marriages among Muslims, the holder of this office used to get Rs. 3 on an average annually.
Rs.	18	Total income per annum.

Expenses

Rs.	8	Annual payment to the Patil and Kulkarni on account of the *hugi* (harvest).
Rs.	4½	Expenditure incurred on account of Moharram and the supply of oil, etc. to the mosque.
Rs.	12½	

On deducting the annual expenditure of Rs. 12½ from the annual income of Rs. 18, a profit of Rs. 5½ went to Mohi-ud-din and his brother Mulla Imam who had a claim to a half share of the profit. Thus the actual profit that Mohi-ud-din got was only Rs. 2-12-0.

For substantiating the claim to the above inam land, Mohi-ud-din produced 7 *sanads* or documents. All the 7 documents are in Persian.

1. The original *sanad* was given by Aurangzeb to Shaikh Daud, son of Shaikh Raje. He belonged to the 14th generation before Mohi-ud-din.
2. The original *sanad* was regranted by Siyad Khan, the Killedar of Aurangzeb, to Shaikh Daud, son of Shaikh Raje.
3. The original *sanad* was again regranted by Alaf Khan, the Killedar of Aurangzeb, to Shaikh Daud, son of Shaikh Raje.
4. Same as the 3rd one. But the word "regranted" is not used. It was simply granted.

5. The original *sanad* granted by Mayin-ud-din, the Killedar of Aurangzeb, to Shaikh Daud, son of Shaikh Raje.
6. The *Sanad* granted by Kalandar Khan, the Killedar of Aurangzeb, to Maujan Khan Mulla, who was the brother of Mohi-ud-din belonging to the 11th generation before the present occupant of the office, whose name also is Mohi-ud-din.
7. Letter of warning given in A.D. 1713 by Mohammad Nazar, the Killedar of Mahmad Shah Gazi, to Wall Mahmad, who belonged to the 13th generation before the present Mohi-ud-din.

In these Persian *sanads* Malapur is said to have been a village in Pargana Nasirabad alias Dharwad belonging to Sarkar Bankapur of Suba Dar-ul-Jaffar Bijapur.

The functions of the Mulla included officiating at the celebration of the Muharam, officiating at the marriage ceremonies of the Muslims, and supplying oil to the mosques for burning lamps in them.

The *Kaifiyat* highlights the following points:

1. The office of Mulla was hereditary.
2. The Mulla performed mainly three functions (see above).
3. For performing his functions satisfactorily —
    - (i) he received an inam land, sometimes a judi-inam, from the Government;
    - (ii) he received annually a fixed grant (in cash) from the Government for officiating at the celebration of the Muharram.
    - (iii) he received from the Muslims some honorarium for officiating at their marriage ceremonies.

(4) The lands were of three kinds : dry, wet and garden lands or mango groves.

(5) The lands were measured in terms of *visas* or *annas*, *beles*, and *pattis*. A *patti* was equivalent to a *guntha* and consisted of 16 *annas* or 8 *beles*.

(6) The payment of rent was either in rupees or in *varahas*.

(7) The Mulla was one of the Balutedars.

(8) The East India Company also recognised the right to inheritance of this office with its inam lands and perquisites.

(9) The grant of inam land was confirmed by every new Killedar, the officer in charge of Kille Dharwad.

(10) The income from the office belonged to the family, not to the individuals. It was shared among brothers.

According to a third *Kaifiyat* a certain Iranagauda, son of Sanganagauda, and grandosn of Linganagauda Patil was enjoying a land measuring 6 *beles* and one *visa* in Hosayellapur, a village of Taluka Dharwad (but now a suburb of Dharwad) as an inam land for his office of Patil. In this land a piece of one *bele* was wet (*tari*) land, and the rest was dry. There were no mango trees in it.

Although this land was originally granted as an inam land to one of the forefathers of Iranna, part of it had now become the *judi* land, for which he was paying Rs. 175-13-0 as *judi* tax, Iranna inherited this land during the Company's rule. He had been enjoying it for 15 years.

In this land of 6 *beles* and one *visa*, a stream was formed in due course, on account of which one *kurgi* of land became waste.

Iranna had given 3 *beles* of land to a ryot for cultivation on *lavani* terms for Rs. 80, and the remaining land Iranna was himself cultivating out of which he got an income of Rs. 96. Thus in all he got an average income of Rs. 176 every year. Deducting the *judi* tax of Rs. 175-3-0. the net profit of three *annas* only went to Iranna. Including other perquisites, Iranna got a profit of Rs. 46-7-0 as shown below:

(1)	Rs. 0-3-0	Profit from land, as mentioned above.
(2)	Rs. 25-0-0	Income from *hutagi*
(3)	Rs. 18-0-0	From Mohatarfa or shop tax
(4)	Rs. 2-0-0	From Jukayi people regarding *lavani.*
(5)	Rs. 0-8-0	From Mahars in lieu of leather footwear.
(6)	Rs. 0-12-0	Perquisites on the occasion of the celebration of the Nagapanchami festival in lieu of jaggery, etc.
	Rs. 46-7-0	

Out of this amount Iranna had to give a share of Rs. 9-1-6 to his brother Basannagauda from land and *Mohatarfa*, and the remaining amount of Rs. 37-5-6 was the net income or profit of Irannagauda.[1]

1. KJ: 1597, *Kaifiyat* No. 32, dated A.D. 1844.

III

Land Revenue System

Types of Land

There were mainly four types of soil, namely, *ragadi* (black), *kemman* (red), *masab* (dark loam with sand), and *gonikal* (gravely land). This classification was made on the basis of the quality of the soil. Another classification was on the basis of the availability of water supply, namely, *patti, kul, thal* and *hakkal.* Patti was again a sloping land with a definite extent of area. It could also be a measure of land varying with different qualities of soil. Of dry lands it contained from two to twelve *Kurgis*, of moist lands from one and a half to eight *Kurgis*. A Kul land was land fed by a tank, a reservoir, especially a large piece of water formed by damming up a valley or hollow between hills into which water flows and is there retained. [1] A *thal* sometimes meant a sugar-cane plantation.[2] It was probably fed by wells or tanks manually built. Another general classification was into wet lands, dry lands and mango groves.

Land holdings were often dictated by the availability of different types of lands in the villages. They were also governed by the economic position of the holders. In some areas, especially the middle portion of the Savanur principality, the best lands were called *chali* lands. They were capable of being taxed to the maximum, hence they were of the best type. The other types of lands could not be taxed to the maximum in relation to their extent, hence they were of a lower type. In other words, from the tax rate, their fertility and type could be determined. Originally, of course while fixing the land tax the fertility of the land, the type of the soil, the availability of water supply and such other factors must have

1. Wilson's *Glossary*, p. 301.
2. *Ibid.*, p. 518.

been taken into consideration. In the middle region the rich members of the society held the best, *i.e. chali* lands, paying the maximum land tax for them. But invariably every *chali* landholder held some lower types of lands as well, such as *Khanda-guttige* and *Makta-guttige* or even *Natta-Kaul* lands. The *chali* landholders were the proprietor-peasants. They were like the Mirasdars and Thalkaris. The rate of taxation for the *chali* lands was usually 10.5 *hons* per *mar* of land. This rate was usually three or four times more than the rate for the second type of land or the *Khanda-guttige* land. The rate of *Khanda-guttige* lands was usually 2.5 *hons* per *mar*, but sometimes more than this rate. For *Makta-guttige* lands the rate was 1.5 *hon* per *mar*, while for *Natta-kaula* it was just 1.00 *hon* per *mar*. In the northern part of the Southern Maratha Country there was apparently a different type of landholding system. The lands of a village were arranged in various groups called *chigars*. Each *chigar* consisted of different qualities of land such as *gadde* or *bagayit*, *beddalu* or *jirayit* and garden lands or *tota* or mango groves or *amrayi*. This arrangement was made probably for benefitting the members of the higher echelons in society who had held the best type of lands paying the highest tax for them. Even the highest tax they could easily pay, as they had the best type of lands. But at the same time they held *khandaguttige* and *khandamakta* lands paying less tax. On the whole they were the gainers. But the middle class and poor people like Balutedars and untouchables had to pay a heavy tax, the latter even if they had no lands. Most of the *Chali* landholders where also Inamdars holding inam lands paying either quit-rent or no rent at all. These were generally the Watandars and office bearers. The members of the ruling class were, as a rule, Brahmins or Marathas coming originally from Maharashtra or only the rich Brahmins from the local areas

Again from the Vijayangara times onwards the land tax went on increasing. The original Vijayanagara tax together with the cesses or imposts was consolidated into the standard tax by the Bijapur Adilshahs called *asl* or *raqam*. The Vijayanagar standard land tax was called *rayarekhe* and the Adilshahi standard rates continued to be in existence even later on under the Nawabs of Savanur, although Majid Khan Dilerjang Bahadur and his Diwan Alikhan introduced another standard land assessment called *ainati*. This rate also continued to be in force along with the above two. There were thus three standard land assessments in the Savanur principality. As these rates were supposed to be very moderate, some of them were, especially during the administration of Diwan Hatim Khan, doubled and even trebled. As a result, only a few, if at all, could pay this enhanced land tax, and in most of the cases only a portion, usually the original amount, of the tax was paid by the people, the rest being treated as in arrears. The rains failed often and the famines were caused. With the increase in the population, the number of tenants-at-will increased. The migrations from one place to another in search of fresh lands and livelihood increased. All this resulted in marking off a class of tillers and landless workers such as *mujariyan* and the big land holders or peasant proprietors such as chali holders and chigar holders. Inamdars and the parasitic official class claimed a share of the produce from the actual tillers of the soil. All this gradually led to the concentration and accumulation of money, especially the surplus money, in the hands of the rich landed elements while balutedars, poor peasant proprietors who were not *Chali* holders, the mujariyan and other landless workers had to part with the fruits of their labour, that is, the produce of the land under their cultivation more and more. The official class, mostly consisting of Brahmins and some Marathas, exploited the peasantry mercilessly exacting from them all manner of imposts such as *masala* fees, *ghasdana*, *Shahupatti*, *tashrif* etc. A large number of cesses have been noted.

Again there were a number of mathas, both Brahmin and Lingayat, and other religious institutions which enjoyed rent-free lands paying only a quit-rent. Added to this an enormous number of Brahmins, not to speak of Muslim Fakirs and Lingayat priests, were the recipients of *varshasanas* at the hands of the rulers, and a sizable portion of the wealth in the royal treasury was spent in paying these *varshasanas* only. There might have been some genuine and deserving cases in such a huge list, and in some cases this practice must have really promoted the religious or spiritual interest of the people. But, by and large, this body of Brahamins, some of them having their own lands, must have been a parasitical class engaged in unproductive activities This must have aggravated the economic imbalance in the society

Patterns of landholdings

Coming to the agrarian system, we find that in respect of the patterns of landholding, land tenures, methods of land assessment and the like, the Vijayanagara traditions provided the base on which the superstructure was built combining the features drawn from the systems prevalent under the later rulers.

Under Vijayanagara the unit of land was known by the term *mar*, and since a certain Venkataraya was the governor of this area, the unit came to be called *Venkatarai mar*. Although there were some measuring rods under Vijayanagara such as *Rajavi-bhadana Kol, Gandaragandana Kol,* etc., these were not used in many parts of the empire. There the areas were measured or the extent of the lands fixed according to the traditional methods. One such method was to demarcate the area of the land by sowing it with a seed-drill drawn by a pair of bullocks. The area that could be sown like this in one day was styled '*Kurgi*' as the seed-drill in the local language was known as *kurgi*. This was really the unit of area measurement. And in a *mar*, whose extent varied from region to region, there were from 12 to 20 kurgis of land. Later under the British rule a kurgi was equivalent to 4 acres, and from the Modi documents of the 18th century (*Nargund Pujari Daftar*) we come to know that a *mar* in the Malaprabha region was equal to 36 bighas.

The lands in the Dharwad region were classified under four heads viz., *pattya. kul, thal* and *hakkal*. The pattya lands got ample water supply from rains. Such lands we find both in mallad and *bailsime* regions, but mostly in the *mallad* area. Similarly the *kul, thal* and *hakkal* lands were found mostly in the *bailsime*, but the mallad area, wherever there was an elevated ground, also had these types. The *kul* lands were fed by the tank water, and the *thal* lands by the reservoirs of water formed between the hills probably by raising *bunds* joining the two hills. The *hakkal* lands were barren lands, having no water-supply either from the tanks or from improvised water reservoirs, but mainly depending on rain water. Even the rain water could not be used effectively as the land was least fertile.

Originally under Vijayanagara most of the lands in this region were tilled by the proprietor-cultivators Probably more lands were available for cultivation and the land tax was comparatively light. Such proprietor-cultivators came to be known in later years as the *Chali* land-holders. These were comparable to the Mirasdars elsewhere. The best lands came to be called *Chali* lands, not on the basis of their fertility — although it meant the same in the last analysis — but on the taxable capacity of the land. As only the best lands could afford to yield the highest produce making it possible for the government to tax them heavily, the *Chali* lands really signified the best lands. But the term *Chali* is better applied to the tenure of land in which the proprietors paid the highest amount of tax for their lands. Thus in the Malaprabha region the tax on *Chali* land was about 10 hons per *mar* while on other lands it was much less, say either 2.50 hons, or 1.50 hons or even 1 hon per *mar*.

According to the Patrak of Mauje Chikkop in Tarf Ramdurg dated A.D. 1810, there were 50 cultivators in Chikkop holding among themselves 71 *mars* (2556 *bighas*) of land by four types of land tenures.

The first type, as mentioned above, was *Chali* tenure. Out of 71 *mars* of land only 7⅛ *mars* were held by the *Chali* holders, but they paid the maximum tax for them. This can be better understood by comparing it with the next tenure called the *Guttige* tenure. By this *Guttige* tenure 44¼ mars of land were held. For 7⅛ *mars* of *Chali* lands 74-3-1-0 *hons* were paid as the tax, while for 44¼ *mars* of *guttige* lands only 98-1-0-0 *hons* were paid. In other words, the rate of taxation for *chali* lands was over 10 hons per *mar* while for *guttige* lands it was a little over 2 hons per *mar*.

The distribution of landholding in this village in 1810 was as follows:

Chali	*Guttige*	*Makta*	*Kaul*
33	43	9	5

Of these *Chali* holders 31 also held *guttige* lands. Of the 43 *guttige* holders 31 were also the *chali* holders, and the remaining 12 were the *guttige* holders. Out of the 9 *makta* holders, 3 were also the *chali* holders, and 6 were *makta* holders. Out of 5 *kaul* holders, 4 were also *chali* holders and one *kaul* holder.

In other words 33 *chali* holders included
31 *guttige* holders
3 *makta* holders
4 *kaul* holders

These 31 *guttige* holders also included 3 *makta* holders and 4 *kaul* holders.

In other words again out of 33 *chali* holders —

1 was the holder of *chali, guttige makta* and *kaul* lands;
2 were the holders of *chali, guttige* and *makta* lands;
3 were the holders of *chali, guttige* and *kaul* lands;
25 were holders of *chali* and *guttige* lands; and
2 were the holders of only *chali* lands.

Out of 50 landholders, 43 were *guttige* holders, of whom 31 were also *chali*-holders and only 12 *guttige*-holders. Among these 12, only one had *kaul* lands as well, and another had *makta* lands as well. In other words, only 10 were purely *guttige* landholders.

Among the remaining 7 non-*guttige* holders, 2 had only *chali* lands, and 5 had only *makta* lands. These latter 5 were purely *makta* landholders, they having no *chali*, nor *guttige* nor *kaul* lands.

There were no purely *kaul* landholders. 4 landholders had *kaul* lands, along with other lands.

	Out of the 71 mars of land	The tax from them was 203-2-1-0 hons
7-0-2-0	were *chali* lands	74-3-1-0 hons
44-1-0-0	were *chali, guttige* lands	98-1-0-0 hons
13-2-0-0	were *makta* lands	22-2-0-0 hons
6-0-2-0	were *kaul* lands	8-0-0-0 hons respectively.

Among the above 50 landholders, only 9 had 3 or more than 3 *mars* of land each, of whom only 3 had 4 or more than 4 *mars* of land. Of these only one had 5 *mars* of land. These 9 landholders paid varying amounts of money as land tax for different types of land they had. These landholders could be arranged as follows, in a descending order according to the quantity of land they held:

Sr. No.	Quantity of land	Tax assessed
1.	5 *mars*	12-3-0-0 *hons*
2.	4-2-0-0	4-2-0-0
3.	4-0-0-0	13-3-0-0
4.	3-3-2-0	6-1-3-1
5.	3-3-0-0	3-3-0-0
6.	3-2-0-0	10-3-2-0
7.	3-2-0-0	15-0-0-0
8.	3-1-0-0	9-1-2-0
9.	3-0-2-0	6-1-0-0

But the man who paid the maximum amount of tax (15-1-2-0) had 2-0-2-0 *mars* of land. His name was Irappa Menasgi. He held 0-3-0-0 mars of Chali land, 1-1-2-0 mars of guttige land, in all 2-0-2-0 mars. The man (Nana Auravadi) who paid 15-0-0-0 hons had 3-2-0-0 mars of makta land. But this seems to be an exception, for in other cases of makta land we find only 1 hon assessed for 2-2-0-0 mars, and 1-2-0-0 for 2 mars. The rate for *makta* lands seems to be 0-3-0-0 per mar, which gives us 1-2-0-0 for 2 *mars*. The rate for *chali* lands was 10-2-0-0 per mar. For guttige lands, there was no fixed rate. It fluctuated widely. One finds, for example, 1 *hon* per mar, 4-2-0-0 hons per *mar*, 6 hons for 1-2-0-0 *mars*, 4 *hons* for 2 *mars*, and 7-2-0-0 *hons* for 4-2-0-0 *mars*. For *kaul* lands, roughly 1 hon was charged per *mar*.

Under serial Nos. 2 and 3 we find wide variations. Under 2 for 4½ mars of guttige land, 4½ hons were charged, the rate being 1 hon *per mar*.

But under 3, for only 4 *mars* 13-3-0-0 hons are charged, the difference being caused by ½ a *mar* of *chali* lands, and by the high amount of 6 hons for only 1½ guttige lands.[1] By and large, the *Chali* lands were the best lands and were most heavily taxed. Next the *guttige* lands and *makta* lands came in a descending order in respect of fertility, but the rates of assessment fixed were not rigid, sometimes the makta lands being taxed more heavily than the guttige lands. The kaul lands were of course the least fertile lands and hence taxed very lightly.

The term *chawar* was used in Taluka Chikodi in 1773[2]. In another document[3] of A.D. 1777 one finds how the Adilshahi tradition continued even into the 18th century. For the unit of land the term *"Idalshahi Chawar"* is used.[4] In 1777 in Mauje Goravinahal of Qasba Manoli in Prant Hukkeri there were 8 Idalshashi Chawars of land. From this the following lands were deducted on account of reasons given against them:

Bighas	**Grantees**
60	granted to Bastawada
60	granted to Godwade
60	granted to Arjunwada
315	granted to Mai Murud
15	To temples
210	To Inamdars
720 Bighas or 6 Chawars (Total)	

These were all alienated lands. The remaining 2 chawars were the lands of the peasants. Of these 2 chawars, ½ were chali lands and 1½ were held by tenancy tenure. The rate of land tax for the *chali* lands was 3 rupees per bigha, and that for khand lands was 2.22 rupees per bigha. Thus only 25% of the lands of the village belonged to the peasants, the 75% being enjoyed by the Inamdars. And even for these khalsa lands of the peasants 556.25 rupees were realised as land tax. This shows how the peasants were exploited by the landed proprietors and Inamdars of the village.[5] In 1680 when Bagalkot was under the rule of Aurangzeb there were in all 210 villages in Bagalkot.[6]

1. KJ: 241 : 353.
2. KJ: 349 : 289.
3. KJ: 1095 : 296.
4. *Ibid.*
5. KJ: 1095 : 296.
6. KJ: 376 : 143.

An important document called Akar Jamabandi of Qasba Konnur in Mamla Torgal of Taluka Nargund dated 1785 gives us very valuable statistics about land tax in that Qasba. The total assessment for Qasba Konnur and the 21 villages coming under it was 7790-50 *hons*, and for Qasba proper itself the assessment was 2579-0-1-0 *hons*.

The villages and the revenue assessed for them were as follows:

1.	Qasba Konnur	2579.0625
2.	Mauje Kalhal	473.375
3.	Kurigovanakop	30.50
4.	Chikop	757.25
5.	Anagudi	199.25
6.	Soriban	120.00
7.	Manihal	296.125
8.	Huligop	93-00
9.	Gonnagar	470.00
10.	Idagal	208.00
11.	Mulangi Khurd	82.50
12.	Aralikate	56.50
13.	Bennur	51.875
14.	Karadgi	81.9375
15.	Tadasi Budruk	84.75
16.	Sangal	1025.25
17.	Lakamapur	40.00
18.	Talakwad	88.125
19.	Barnur	162.625
20.	Wasan	199.25
21.	Dongar-Govinakop	133.125
22.	Kalapur	384.25
		7590.25

[But in the document the total given is 7790.50 *hons*]

As mentioned above, the assessment for Qasba Konnur proper was 2579-0-1-0 hons, of which 908-2-1-0 *hons* came from 86-0-1-2 mars of land held by the peasants. Of these peasants' lands, 14-1-3-0 were held by *Chali* tenure, the rate of assessment being 20.79. There were in all 6 land tenures. The lands held by these tenures and their rates of assessment can be shown as under:

Tenure (type)	lands (*mars*)	Assessment rate (*hons*)
1. *Chali*	14-1-3-0	20.79
2. *Kat-gutta*	35-2-1-2	9.21
3. *Horsut*[1]	15-2-2-2	2.78
4. *Nat-gutta*	12-0-1-0	6.13
5. *Makta-gutta*	6-3-1-2	8.036
6. *Hul-kaul*[2]	1-2-0-0	5.166

The assessment from Qasba Konnur proper from different sources can be shown as under:

Amount (hons)	Source	Land (*mars*)
908-2-1-0	*Khalsat* lands from peasant	86-0-1-2
160-0-0-0	Kamal Nagnur	10-0-0-0
1232-1-0-0	Judi Inamdars	217-3-0-0
96-3-0-0	Baluta Mohtarfa	-----
182-2-0-0	Set Sanadi	45-3-2-0
Total: 2579-0-1-0		359-2-3-2

Similarly for all the remaining 21 villages we get both the assessment and the quantity of lands.

Now a comparison of these rates in different villages can be made as under:

Rates (per *mar*)

Village	Chali	Kat-gutta	Makta	Nat-kaul	Hor-sut	Hul-kaul
Konnur	20.79	9.21	8.036	6.13	2.78	5.166
Kalahal	11.00		8.60			
Kurigovinakop	12.00		6.84	6.22		
Chikop	12.00	9.80				
Manihal	10.00	2.92		8.00		
Idagal	12.00					
Mulangi Khurd	7.00					
Wasan	8.00		8.2			6.08
Dongaragovankop	8.00					
Sureban				11.00		
Karadgi			7.59	8.14		
Sangal			8.75		6.58	

1. Lease of waste lands.
2. Lease of grass lands.

In the regions north of the Ghataprabha there was a different kind of classification and grouping of lands. The unit of land was not a *mar* nor *kurgi* nor even a bigha or chavar, but what was known as a *chigar*.

There were six types of land. The first was the garden land, land producing the most valuable kinds of crops, as sugar-cane, pepper, ginger, etc.[1] The *raqam* or the land assessment for the first type of land was 20 *hons* per chigar, that for the second type was 19 *hons*, that for the 3rd 13 *hons*, that for fourth 2.50 *hons*, that for the fifth 6 hons, and that for the sixth 2 *hons*.

The names of the six types of lands were *Ragada, Nadi-sete, Melgai (Malegai), Masar, Bag and Amarai* respectively.

In Pargana Murgod also the lands came to be measured in terms of *Chigars* later on, although in the 17th and 18th centuries the *mar* was the unit of measurement. A document entitled Jaminzada of Mauje Budnur budruk in Pargana Murgod gives the following details about the land system in that village.

There were 32 *chigars* of land in this village. Their distribution was as follows:

Chigars	***Particulars***
5 0.0.0	Common lands
1.3 0.0	With temples
0.2.0.0	With religious places
0.1.0.0	Additional Inamdars
3.0.0.0	With Jamidars of Mahals
12.3.2.0	With Watandars of the village
2.1.1.0	With local militia
0.3.3.0	Fallow land
26.2.2 0	

The position of the remaining 5.1.2.0 lands was as follows:

2.1.3.0	*Chali* lands with the peasants
2.3.3.0	*Gutaga* lands held by the peasants.
	Of these *Gutaga* lands 2.1.3.0 were *gutaga* lands held by the peasants, and 0.2.0.0 were held by Sri Divakar Dikshit.

1. Wilson, 323.

The common lands were not situated in one place but were scattered in the hamlets and other places, some of them being probably waste lands and the lands covered by the boundaries. The Jamidars of Mahals were Desai Chanchikar, Deshpande and Nadgauda. The Watandars were the Gramjoshi and Judi Inamdars. The Sarvamanya lands were enjoyed by the Naik, Patil, Kulkarni and Talawar. The temples to which the lands were granted were those of Sri Hanamant, Yellawa, Ramalinga, Lakshmi and Gramadevi. The *dharmadav* lands were alienated to Krishnabhat Joshi and Sripatbhat Gokak.

The lands thus alienated, including those granted to local militia, amounted to 26.2.2.0 *chigars*; which constituted a major portion of the total lands (32 *chigars*) of the village. The remaining 5.1.2.0 *chigar* lands were held by *chali* and *gutaga* tenures.

From a Taleland of Mauze Badani, P/Lakshmeshwar, Pram Karnatak[1] dated 1813, we know that the *pattya* were lands of definite extent coming under any type such as *chali, Khandagutga, kaul* and even miscellaneous land. In this village of Badni there seem to have been 5 *patya* or *pattis* of *chali* land paying 991-875 rupees of land tax, which means that the tax for each patti was Rs. 198.375. There were 8.25 *pattis* of *khand-gutka* land paying Rs. 351. 5625, which means that the tax for each patti of this type of land was 42.6136, and the tax for *chali* land was about five times as much as the tax on *khand-gutka* land. The *pattis* of *kauli* land were 5.75 and the tax for all these was 121.875 rupees, which gives us the rate of 21.195 per *patti*. We have now rates of taxation for the above three types of land:

Rs. 198 and odd for *chali* land of one *patti*.

Rs. 42 and odd for *khandgutka* land of one *patti*.

Rs. 21 and odd for *kauli* land of one *patti*.

This would mean that the tax on the *chali* land was the highest and was four times or 4½ times as much as the tax on *khandgutka* lands, and the *khandgutka* tax was double that of the kauli land tax. The *kauli* land tax was just 21 and odd rupees per *patti* while the *Chali* tax was 198 and odd rupeees. We might recall that in the village of Chikkoppa the rate of taxation for *chali* lands was 10.5 hons. per *mar*, that for the *khandgutka* land was 2.5 hons and for the *nattakaul* land it was just 1.00 *hon*. Here also the ratio was that the *chali* tax was about 4½ or 5 times as much as the *khandgutka* tax, and the *khandgutka* tax was double the *kaul* tax. Hence it appears that the *patti* was equivalent to a *mar*, and that *patti* and *mar* were synonyms.

1. KJ: 554 : 523.

It is also significant to notice here that the lands themselves are called in the documents the *chali* land or the *khandgutka* land or the *kauli* land.

A document, *Hiseb zamin-zada of Mauza Devagodanakati from Pargana Ranebidnur*[1] dated A.D. 1803 speaks of two types of lands, namely, *ragada* or black, and *tambadi* or red. Of the latter a sub-variety was loam mixed with sand called *masab*. In this village of Devagodanakati there were in all 33 *pattis* of lands. Of these, 9 were ragad or black and 24 were *tambadi* or red. From these lands the following were being enjoyed by grantees such as temples, Lingayat priests called Jangams, Inamdars, Thikandars and local militia called *Setsanadi*.

	Grantee	**Lands in pattis**		
1.	Temple	1	(red)	-
2.	Jangam	½	(red)	-
3.	a. Desai (sarvamanya)	1	-	(black)
		1	-	(black)
		1	(red)	-
	b. Vadgir Mahajan	1	-	(black)
	sarvamanya	1	-	(black)
		1	(red)	-
	c.	1	-	(black)
		1	(red)	-
4.	Thikandar	½	(red)	
		1	-	(black)
		1	(red)	
		1	(red)	
		1	(red)	
5.	Setsanadi	½	-	(black)
		3	(red)	
		18½	(12 + 6½)	

Thus 18½ pattis were the alienated lands, out of which 6½ were black and 12 were red. The remaining 14½ were the *khalsa* lands:

The followign are the details of the *khalsa* lands.

6½	-	waste, uncultivated
1	-	under cultivation (*lavani*)
1	-	waste
8¾	-	under cultivation (*lagvad*)

1. KJ: 199.

To the khalsa lands of 14½ *pattis* were added the following:

Judimanya Inamdars	7	pattis
from Setsanadi	1½	
	23	

The details of the 23 *pattis* of land are as follows

8	waste lands
14¾	under *lagvad* (cultivation)
23 Total	

Details of 14¾ *pattis*:

8¾	*pattis-khalsa*
4½	*pattis*-Judi Inamdar
1½	*pattis*-Setsanadi
14¾	

The *ainat* of lands also is given.

For Desai Sarvamanya lands —

For 2 *pattis* of *regad* land 7½ *hons* were *ainat*

For 1 *patti* of *masab* land 3 *hons* were *ainat*

For Nadgir land —

Patti	Type of land	Hons.	Land Tax
2	*ragad*	6	*ainat*
1	*masab*	3	*ainat*

For Patil —

1	*regad*	10	*ainat*
2	*masab*	20	*ainat*

For Thikandars —

1	*regad*	6	*ainat*
1	*masab*	6	*ainat*

For Setsanadi —

½	*regad*	5	*ainat*
3	*masab*	7	*ainat*

For 14¾ *pattis* of land

patti		*ainat*
khalsa	8¾	71½
Judi Inamdar	4½	32
Setsanadi	1½	7½

Some details of 83/4 lands were :

patti	*ainat*
8 old	(701–)
1/4 waste	0-1-2-1 (1 =)

For 14¾ *pattis* 1½ hons are given as *ainat.*

The deductions are:

For *khalsa* 38-0-2-0 *hons*

Details are :

2 *hons* on account of *kaul*, 32.2.2.0 on account of *khandmakta* and *Kor* Tagar 3½ on account of *Matvani.*

It seems that the loss due to *khandmakta* was much more than the loss due to *kaul* and *natvani.* The lowest *ainat* was for Desai and Nadgir *sarvamanya* lands and it was about 3 *hons* per *patti* of land, whether *regad* or *masab*. For Patil it was 10 *hons* per *patti*. For *Thikandars* it was 6. For khalsa it was about 9, for *judi* Inamdar about 8, and for Setsanadi about 7.

In the Dambal area[1] the usual four tenures, namely, *chali, kutguta, khandmakta* and *kaul* were in vogue. In Qasba Gadag there were 159 *kuls* and 167 ploughs in A.D. 1824. But in 1825 there were 160 *kuls* and 164 ploughs. In all there were 130.0625 *mars* of land in Qasba Gadag which were equivalent to 780.375 *kurgis* of land, which means that one *mar* of land was exactly equal to 6 *kurgis* of land. These lands were held by 5 tenures as follows:

Tenures	Extent of lands	Rate of tax per mar
Chali	26.1875 *mars*	79.246
Katguta	13.1875 *mars*	20.372
Khandmakta	60.1875 *mars*	20.708
Nangar Kaul	30.25 *mars*	4.371
Kor	00.25 *mars*	63.00
	130.0625 *mars*	

Thus there were 130.0625 *mars* of land in Qasba Gadag, which were equivalent to 780.375 *kurgis* of land, and the total land tax for all these lands was 3738.531 hons or rupees.

From the Zamin-zada of Mauze Atikati, Majare Pawapur, Ramapur, P/Murgod, Taluka Manoli dated 1777 we get the following details:[2]

The total number of lands in this village was 44-1-2-0 chigars. Of these 30 were *regad* (black) and 14-1-2-0 were *masab* (red). From these

1. KJ: 177.
2. KJ: 462.

2-2-2-0 were deducted on account of habitation, hills etc. giving us a balance of 41-3-0-0 chigars.

	41-3-0-0	
Less	18-2-0-0	On account of temple, GramJoshi, Inamdar, Judimanya. etc.
	23-1-0-0	balance
	23-1-0-0	
Less	8-0-2-0	On account of recruitment and maintenance of military forces lying idle, etc.
	15-0-2-0	Balance under cultivation (*lavani*) as shown below:
	3-0-1-0	Chali
	7-1-1-0	Gutga
Less	3-3-0-0	Kaul
	1-0-0-0	Kor
	0-0-0-0	Balance Nil

The Wahiwat of Mauje Badni, Taluka Savanur[1] dated 1812 gives us a glimpse into the land system of that village. The revenue collection of the year including the arrears of the previous year was 1236-2-2-1 rupees. The arrears of last year were collected family-wise. While giving the details of Ain Jama of the current year, the document gives the land revenue, etc.:

Lands	***Extent in mars***	***Tax***
Chali	5-0-0-0	110-0-0-0
Kadguta	6-1-0-0	47-3-0-0
Kauli	10-2-0-0	54-3-0-0-0
	21-3-0-0	212-2-0-0
	Plus	63-3-0-0
		276-0-3-0

The sum of 63-3-0-0 *hons* was collected from miscellaneous taxes, such as quit-rent from Inamdars, *mohtarfa*, customs duties, etc. From the total of 276-0-3-0 hons, a sum of 58-2-3-0 was deducted on account of village incidental expenses, bringing the total down to 217-2-0-0 *hons.* When converted into rupees at the rate of 3-3-0-0 per *hon*, it comes to 815-2-2-0 rupees. To this sum of 815-2-2-0 rupees the following additions were made. 17-0-3-0 Rupees on account of extra collected.

1. KJ: 554 : 512

287-2-1-1 Rupees recovered from the loans. Total Rs. 1120-1-2-1. This is the total collection of the current year (1812 A.D.) When the arrears of Rs. 116-1-0-0 recovered for the last year are added, we get the final total of Rs. 1236-2-2-1.

Among the above lands of 21-3-0-0 mars, 0-1-0-0 *chali* lands were under *Kaul*.

0-2-0-0	khandmakta lands were under Chali
0-2-0-0	kor lands were under khandmakta

The above analysis shows how the land revenue dwindles when the lands lie waste, or when the chali lands are granted on favourable terms as kaul lands or kor lands are granted as khandmakta lands.

There is a very useful table in Modi in the Pune Archives[1] giving us minute details about the landholders of Qasba Haveri in 1795, their holdings, the type of the lands held, the tax assessed on them, the deductions, if any, and the like, under 84 columns.

There are in all 81 landholders and the total land is 17.75 mars. There were 4 types of land, namely, *gadde, bagayit, regad* and *masab*. Two types of *tenures*, chali and khandguta are mentioned. Of these 81 landholders, only one, namely, Fakirappa Shilavant, held 5.25 kurgis or 31-5 bighas of land. Next to him, only 3 persons held lands measuring more than 18 bighas, namely, Malya Devgiri (22.5 bighas), Basya Devgiri (18 bighas and 11.25 pands) and Kanchana gauda (24 bighas and 3.75 pands).

We also get tax rates of different types of lands. For 8.43 bighas of chali lands, the tax was 15 hons. For 6.75 bighas the tax was 27 hons, for 3 kurgis and 4.5 bighas the tax was 39 hons. Again for 1.5 kurgi the tax was 15 and also 19.50 hons. Thus do we find that there was no fixed rate for all chali lands, which means that all chali lands were not of the same quality. This would only mean that they were taxed to the maximum. But the rate of *patti* was the same in all the cases. It was double the *ain*. For example, out of 15, 5 was the ain and 10 was the *patti*.

For the bagayit lands, the taxes for some lands may be noted. For 6.75 bighas of land 27 hons were the tax. For 5.06 bighas 21 hons were the tax, and for 4.5 bighas 9 hons were the tax. But, for 2.5 bighas 12 hons were charged. Here also the tax rate varied with the quality of the lands.

---

1. KJ: 177 : 352.

For the *gadde* lands the taxes were as follows:

	For 4.5 bighas	9 hons
	For 2.25 bighas	6 hons
Again	For 4.5 bighas	6 hons

So here also the rate varied with the quality.

For the *regad* lands the tax was —

	For 4.5 bighas	9 hons
	For 18 bighas	10 hons
	For 27 bighas	36 hons
	For 9 bighas	12 hons
Again	For 9 bighas	15 hons

For *masab* lands also we see the same thing:

	For 4.5 bighas	6 hons
Again	For 4.5 bighas	7.5 hons

In Qasba Konnur (in 1785) the rates of assessment in 6 land tenures were as follows:

	Rate per mar (hons)
1. Chali	20 and odd
2. Katgutta	9 and odd
3. Maktagutta	8 and odd
4. Natgutta	6 and odd
5. Hul kaul	5 and odd
6. Horsut (lease of waste land)	2 and odd

Thus although the area was small, yet there were different types of land units and land tenures, the standard land assessment changed from time to time, and there were a number of cesses added to the land tax. Usually the common cultivator was crushed under the weight of taxation whereas the well-to-do agriculturists, the *elite* of the village did not feel the burden much, having many superior lands with them along with the ordinary ones. The Zamindars, the Inamdars, the *mokasa* or *dumala* holders enjoyed partial or total exemption from taxes, while the whole burden fell on the ordinary landholders and tenants.

IV

Trade and Commerce

Urban Centres and Market towns

The Southern Maratha country was essestially a landlocked country, and had to depend upon the western ports for its seaborne trade. The main cash crops were cotton, sugarcane and tobacco. Timber was plentiful in Malenad area. The Southern Maratha country contained a number of urban and commercial centres such as Bagalkot, Kerur, Gokak, Azamnagar, Nargund, Dharwad, Hubli, Annigeri, Gadag, Mishrikoti, Savanur, Bankapur, Haveri, Ranebinnur and the like.

There were few good roads but many pathways or tracks joining commercial centres in this region with the markets within and outside the region. Cotton, sugarcane, tobacco, rice, etc. were sent along these tracks to distant markets. The Lamanis and such other tribes carried the goods over long distances. The textile industry was scattered and widespread. Generally everyone in the cultivator's family in the cotton-growing belts did the spinning in spare time. There were in qasbas and peths such as Dharwad, Hubli, Nargund, Haveri, Havasbhavi etc. many looms working.

Hubli[1] was "one of the most flourishing towns in the Southern Maratha Country". It contained in 1853 according to a survey made by the Company's Govt. 5,458 houses with a population of about 33,000 at the rate of 6 persons per house. It possessed "a number of old established banking and trading firms, and bills of exchange for large amounts are readily obtainable here on Bombay, Madras, and all the large towns of the peninsula."

---

1. For some of the towns, more details are available in the British administrators reports. From them one can say that even in the second decade of the 19th century the position might have been similar. There do not seem to be any drastic changes in this field.

The trade of Hubli chiefly consisted in cotton fabrics manufactured in the town itself or neighbouring villages, grain, oil, ghee, tobacco, betelnuts, chillies etc. Raw cotton was mostly sent to Bombay by way of Kumta. Tobacco, betel-nuts and chillies which were produced in the southern parganas of Hubli were re-exported from Bombay to the interior. The imports of Hubli coming from the coast were mainly salt, metals, British goods, coconuts and the like.[1]

In 1853 the taluka of Navalgund contained the samats of Navalgund, Morab, Rattigwad and Yavgal, the Annigeri Mahal and a part of the jagir of the late Chief of Nippani. The taluka contained 78 villages. Navalgund was in the north-east traversed by the small river Benne, a tributary of the Malaprabha. The water of this stream was too much brackish and not fit for domestic use. Good water was generally scarce in this area. The wells also were few, and the water generally brackish. The only drinking water that the people could get was from the tanks where the rain water collected during the monsoons. In the summer the tanks either dried up or the water was scanty. In times of drought the people suffered much.

Cotton was the chief product of the Navalgund area. There were only two towns here, Navalgund and Annigeri. Women in Navalgund did spinning besides their domestic work, and the yarn spun by them was sold in the market of Hubli.

In 1853 the Havasbhavi division consisted of two Mahals— Tilavalli and Kaginele, the former mostly coming under Mallad area and the latter under Bayalsime. This area was traversed by the Varada river and many streams supplying the tanks. Sugarcane was grown in plenty.

The market towns in the two mahals were Havasbhavi, Tilavalli, Halebail, Chik-Basur, Kusnur, Kalkeri and Kaginele. The market towns in the neighbourhood were Chik-kerur, Shashgiri, Alur, Dumanhal, Haveri, Karajgi, Devihosur, and Budgi. Kusnur produced different varieties of white cloth which was immediately consumed by the local people. The yarn was supplied to Kusnur from Davangere and Devihosur. Some villages produced coarse cloth called Dhangart and Kamblis The fleece for Kamblis was procured from shepherds at Huphunsi and Kerur. "The district possesses little trade beyond what is carried on at the market towns for the consumption of the inhabitants". It, however, exported dried chillies, jaggery, rice and castor oil. From the coast were imported salt, dried coconuts, oil, cloths of British manufacture, etc. From Hubli, Harihar and Dambal came cotton fabrics. There was a road running from Rattihalli to Kumta, and every year about 12,000 bullocks laden

1. *Selections from the Records of Bombay Government,* XII (Bombay, 1853).

with tobacco, cotton, rice and iron went to Kumpta, from Rattihalli, Ranibennur and Kod areas via Tilavalli.

In Tilavalli and some parts of Kaginele sugarcane was grown, out of which coarse sugar and jaggery were made.

In 1853 the abkari revenue from the sale of the juice of the date tree was Rs. 3,310 for the whole taluka. Unfortunately the people did not grow date into full-fledged fruits fit for export nor did they make any attempt at manufacturing sugar from the date fruits which contain a great quantity of saccharine matter. From its leaves mats were made, or they were used for thachting the roofs of houses.

There were many useful tanks in the area such as the Kaginele tank, Hire Lingadahalli tank, the Tilavalli tank, the two Kachvi tanks, the two of Chik-Basur, the Havasbhavi tank etc. besides many wells and ponds.

The trading activities of Mishrikot may be briefly noted. In the north of the Mahal the Budnigud range of hills runs from north-west to south-east over a distance of 8 miles. The western part also is hilly and towards the Kanara border was covered with fine timber-producing forest. It was full of tanks of various sizes. The principal crop was rice. Sugarcane, of the smaller variety, was grown. Rice was an important item of export. The jaggery made from sugarcane was locally consumed.

There were about seven bazars held in the neighbourhood of Mishrikot, *viz.*, Mishrikot, Hulgop, Kudalgi, Kalghatgi, Bommigatti, Tadas and Halyal

At Mishrikot there were about 24 looms in 1853, and 50 rupees worth of coarse cotton cloth was manufactured every week. To the Hulgop bazar came merchants from the plains, from Jamkhandi, Ramdurg etc. for buying rice. In Hulgop 450 families nine-tenths of the whole population, were employed in cleaning rice from husk. Again at Hulgop there were six families of about 40 men employed in iron working: there were six furnaces, employing from five to seven men each. "A furnace turns out about five maunds of iron every week; it is entirely consumed in the neighbourhood. One maund brings about Rs. 1-8-0. The iron is considered to be of bad quality being hard and brittle and unfit for the fabrication of anything but coarse agricultural implements, and pans for boiling sugar."

The Kalghatgi bazar was the most important in the district and was frequented by many merchants coming from the plains, from such places as Ramdurg, Nargund, Bagalkot and Kaladgi. There was a good deal of traffic between Goa and Kalghatgi. The imports from Goa included salt, cocoanut oil, cocoanuts, coir, kashew nuts, katechu, betel-nuts, some of which were exported to Hubli from here. Salt, however, was the most important item of import. About 2000 bullock-loads, containing 5000 maunds of salt worth Rs. 6000 were imported from Goa every year. There was a direct road from Kalghatgi to Goa going through the Diggee Ghat and another, rather a circuitous one, going through Taliwadi Ghat. A loaded bullock took about 10 days for going to Goa from Kalghatgi by the Diggee Ghat, and about 16 days by Taliwadi. The price of salt at the Kalghatgi bazar was Rs. 1-4-0, but in Goa it was just one anna per maund. The Portuguese took the duty of 3 annas on their borders. At Taliwadi 12 annas were taken as duty while it entered the Bombay area and 4 annas for carriage and profit. Thus the total of the money spent on one maund of salt would come to Rs. 1-4-0. One single Sawkar of Kalghatgi imported cloth worth Rs. 100 every month from Hubli and Lakshmeshwar.

At the Bommigatti market besides salt, rice and betel-nut, plantains also were sold About 30 bullock-loads of plantains, worth Rs. 1-10-0 per load, came to Bommigatti every week from Bartanhalli in Kanara. Most of the plantains were sent to the interior from here Salt came from Ankola, and cotton cloth from Hubli and from Arlikatti in the Tadas Mahal.

Trade Routes

Traffic was going on between Mishrikot and 4 ports on the Western coast, *viz.,* Goa Sadashivgad Ankola and Kumpta. A road running from Kalghatgi to Goa via Sambrani and Diggee Ghat was about 105 miles in length. The road running from Kalghatgi to Sadashivgad via Yellapur and the Barbali Ghat was about 40 miles. The road was a mere track. The Ghat was not good. The road ran almost along the Kalinadi and in dry seasons sometimes even in the river bed. The Kali river was navigable upto Mallapur, 14 or 15 miles from the sea.

The regular traffic between Hubli and Kumpta was by a made road via Sirsi, 110 miles in length. The made road from Mundgod to Sirsi and the Nikund Ghat joined Kalghatgi to Kumpta by a track about 100 miles long. The direct route, however, from Kalghatgi to Kumta via Yellapur and the Aribayal Ghat was about 80 miles. This road was a mere track through the jungle, and yet because of its short distance it was frequented by merchants. The road between Kalghatgi and Ankola via Yellapur and the Aribayal Ghat was about 78 miles long.

In the west of this mahal timber was available in plenty : teak, black-wood, *matti, honni* or *hasan*. There was a great demand for logs about 12 feet long, one foot wide and about 4 inches thick. 10 to 12 such logs were carried in a cart and sold at Kalghatgi for about 4½ rupees per load.

Manufactures and Handicrafts

Quite a good number of residents of Badami subsisted by manufactures. The chief manufacturing towns were Kerur and Guledgud. Kerur specialised in the manufacture of sarees which were exported to Pune, Bombay and the Konkan. According to Wingate in 1850 there were 500 looms at Kerur. But owing to rise of prices of cotton, and to the competition with similar goods coming from Gokak, Rabakavi and other towns nearer to the coast, Kerur suffered after 1850. In 1853 (the date of the report) the number of the looms had come down to 350.

In Guledgud, on the other hand, the manufacture of cloths for cholis or boddices was in full swing, there being about 1800 looms in 1853. These clothes were of a high quality, as they contained either a mixture of silk and cotton or entirely silk. Their price varied from Rs. 0-1-0 to Rs. 1-8-0 per *khan* of 20 inches. Generally the English cotton yarn was used. The goods produced by these looms fetched 4 lakh rupees. This cloth was mostly exported to Sholapur, Pune, Konkan and Bombay.

The cotton textiles of Badami and Mudkavi were of coarse variety, unlike those of Guledgud. The money fetched by these manufactures was used for paying the tax and for the imports of cotton yarn, silk, wheat, rice, etc.

The use of English yarns became popular and profitable for the manufacturers of fine cloths, but it threatened to oust the locally made yarn from the field.

A document dated 1827 from the Sheshadri Papers in the Karnataka Archives gives the transit duties levied on goods passing through Manoli by different roads. Manoli was connected with the outside markets by two roads *viz.*, the Torgal Road and the Suladkatti Road, and a river-way, obviously the Malaprabha. The tax was paid in three types of coins, viz. *nava-rokka* (new coins), *juna-rokka* (old coins), and rupees. It also mentions some commercial taxes such as *Phaski*. Oil, husk, etc. were transported on bullocks.

Mohtarfa

A number of commercial taxes were levied, one of them being the mohtarfa. The payers of mohtarfa in this area could be classed under four heads.

(1) shopkeepers, (2) manufacturers and mechanics, (3) weavers, and (4) miscellaneous contributors.

Mohtarfa is an Arabic word, and was used as a general commercial tax in Persian, Telugu, Tamil, Marathi, and Kannad.

It signified a tax or taxes levied on trades and professions, on the artificers of a village or their implements, as upon the weaver's loom, upon tradesmen and their shops and stalls, and sometimes upon houses.[1] However the exact nature of the tax is disputed. According to Dr. Marshall[2] it was a ground rent paid by the people for its use, themselves having no proprietary rights in it. This seems to be an extreme view, although there were some cases in which people paid the tax for getting permission to start their craft or build some structure for their craft on land. Later all manner of exactions came to be included under this head such as the loom tax, the house tax, the shop tax, the tax on oil-pressers and the like.

The Mohtarfa was collected usually in instalments by the local hereditary officials such as the Gauda or Patil and the Shanbhoga or Kulkarni. These tax-collectors were themselves exempted from the payment of the tax. In due course these tax-collectors became part of a privileged class. They came to acquire different privileges, usually with the connivance of higher authorities. Not only were they exempted from the payment of Mohtarfa, but their relatives, and even the occupants or tenants of the houses belonging to these collectors were exempted from this tax. These tenants were also mostly rich traders. For example, in Ranebinnur there were 4 Patils, 2 Kulkarnis and 1 Seth who owned many houses that were rented to rich traders. The Patels owned 59 houses, the Kulkarnis 77 and the Seth 14. As these 150 houses belonged to the above hereditary tax-collectors, almost all of them were exempted from the payment of Mohtarfa. In return for this service of collection of Mohtarfa for the Government, they were hereditarily entitled to certain perquisites which were burdensome to the payers who were engaged in various professions such as weaving and in trade and commerce. For example, they exacted 18 seers of oil yearly from every oil mill.

Generally those who paid the highest amount of Mohtarfa were very rich merchants. They were either bankers, or traders or shopkeepers. Some examples may be given. Nand Naik of Hubli who paid Rs. 115 a year as Mohtarfa was a big Sawkar, owned the best house in Hubli and many shops. In Navalgund a certain trader or Baniya who paid annually Rs. 252.80 as Mohtarfa, had 11 shops and 3 houses. Ser Appa Naik of Belgaum who paid Mohtarfa of Rs. 85 had shops throughout the Deccan, and his yearly profit was Rs. 20,000. A shopkeeper of Gokak who paid Rs. 66 was at once a silk merchant, a jeweller (or shroff) and a bankar (or Sawkar).

1. Wilson's *Glossary*, pp. 350-51.
2. Bombay Archives, RD, 97/1181 of 1840.

The chief products of the weavers in this area were sarees, dupattas and coarse cloth.

In 1840 the total amount of Mohtarfa from the town of Chikodi was Rs. 1297-15-0. This was collected from 350 individuals classed under professions or castes as under:

1. Grocers and grain-sellers chiefly Gujars, Jains and Lingayats.
2. Cloth merchants.
3. Perfumers.
4. Pan sellers and vegetable sellers.
5. Shroffs.
6. Artisans: Smiths, oil-men, dyers etc.
7. Cloth merchants.
8. Miscellaneous payers.

The cotton cleaner or Pinjar came to have an added importance in this area. Their number was small, probably it required some skill and hence they could manage to have the monopoly of cotton cleaning in some places. In Bagalkot a cotton cleaner enjoyed the monopoly of 14 villages, and for this he paid the Mohtarfa of Rs. 177. He was even included in the list of Balutas. His importance suddenly increased with the greater demand for cleaned cotton.

The road system in this area was not encouraging. Even as late as the forties of the 19th century, it was unsatisfactory. The roads that were constructed by using hard material like stones or murum were those between Belgaum and Dharwad, and between Belgaum and the Ram Ghat. Although many cash crops were produced, the cultivator and also the trader suffered for want of good roads. There were of course cart tracks, but it was difficult even to pass small Ghats safely along these tracks. They were then forced to carry their goods in a round about way increasing the cost of production and raising the prices of these goods.

The road running from Bombay southward came only upto Satara, and, as noted already, there was a built road from Belgaum to Dharwad. If the distance between Satara and Belgaum was reduced by joining them by this road, then goods could easily move upto Harihar, Bangalore, Chitradurga and Bellary in the south and up to Kolhapur, Bombay, etc. in the north. There were also no bridges worth the name, and this was another obstacle to the movement of the goods by tracks.

V

Money and Banking

As the trading activities were going on in several parts of the Southern Maratha Country, either in local markets called *Santes* or in large tracts of inland territories or with foreign markets through ports on the western coast, there was an increasing demand for means of exchange. In local markets the barter system was in vogue to some extent. But along with this system the monetary transactions also used to take place. As this area had come under the sway of three major powers, namely, Vijayanagara, Bijapur Sultanate and the Marathas, one finds a medley of coins introduced by all these powers in this area. But the Vijayanagara influence was paramount.

Coins in Circulation

Thus we find a large number of varahas in circulation under different names pertaining to different local affiliations. Of these two are often mentioned in the contemporary documents, namely, *Nilkanthi Varahas* and *Sannageri Varahas*. A varaha was a gold coin bearing some sign (an image of some deity, or a vehicle of the deity, and the like) on the obverse and a legend (generally the name of the king who struck the coin) on the reverse in three horizontal lines. Its weight was usually 52 grains troy. A half varaha was called a *honnu*. Its weight was under Vijayanagara 26 grains troy. Later Shivaji also struck gold coins called *Shivarais* with an increased weight (44 : 12 grains). And these *Shivarais* were also known as *hons*. It became a practice in the post-Vijayanagara and Maratha period to call all the gold varahas hons. Under the Adilshahs the term *hon* was already employed for the standard gold coins and the same practice was later continued by Shivaji in his kingdom.

The varahas minted at Ikkeri, the capital of the Keladi or Bidnur rulers, were called Ikkeri or Ekeri *hons*, and the gold coins minted at Dharwad were known as Dharwadi *hons*. In addition to these, there were Mohurs as well. Among the silver coins Dharwadi, Arcoti and Fulcheri rupees were in circulation.

It may be noted that under Vijayanagara the denominations of the gold coin *varaha* or *gadyana* were the *pratapa* (half-varaha), *kati* or *darana* (one-fourth), rarely *chinna* (one-eighth), *hana* (one-tenth) and *haga* (one-fortieth). The *hana* with its denominations was generally used for small day-to-day transactions. The denominations of the *hana* were *adda* (one-half of the *hana*), *haga* (one-fourth of the *hana*), *bele* (one-eighth of the *hana*), *visa* (one-sixteenth of the *hana*), *arevisa* (one thirty-secondth of the *hana*) and kasu (one-sixty-fourth of the *hana*). Upto the *haga* the coins were of gold. The *visa* was probably a silver coin also called *tara*,[1] and the *kasu* was a copper coin.

As the area of Southern Maratha Country changed hands in the pre-Maratha times from Vijayanagara to Adilshahi Kingdom and *vice versa*, but continued to exist mostly under Bijapur during the later period of the Vijayanagara empire, this area retained the Vijayanagara coinage with certain modifications. Now the unit of coinage, as it came down from Vijayanagara was the *hon* instead of the *varaha*, but it was a *hon* whose value was considerably reduced, which more or less took the place of the *hana* of Vijayanagara times. And this *hon*, as the unit of gold coinage, was later on adopted by the Maratha ruler Shivaji. In the Bijapur Kingdom if the *hon* was the unit of gold coinage, the *rupee* became the unit of silver coinage.

As the Krishna-Tungabhadra Doab later went under the sway of the Marathas, the same coinage was mostly continued by the Peshwas, which we find to some extent in the Southen Maratha Country as well. The denominations of the *hon* under Shivaji and later under the Peshwas were the *pratapa* (one-half of the *hon*), *darana* (one-fourth), *chaval* (one-eighth), *duval* (one-sixteenth), *bele* (one-thirty-secondth), and *visa* (one-sixty-fourth of the *hon*). The hon under Shivaji was a gold coin, but the metal of its denominations we do not know for certain. Probably it was silver down to the visa and the coins denoting its sub-divisions were probably of copper. In the Southern Maratha Country the *chaval, bele, visa, kasu* and *ruka* were found in addition to the *hon*. The *darana* was rarely mentioned. Here the *chaval* was also used along with the *bele* for the one-eighth part of the *hon*, while the *visa*, and *kasu* were one-half and one-fourth of the *chaval* respectively. Although in the Maratha system

1. *Journal of the Royal Asiatic Society*, 1896, p. 344.

the *chaval* was equal to 4 *beles*, here in the Southern Maratha Country it was equal to a bele, following the local traditions. For *darana* another name was probably the *pavali*, which meant one-fourth of the hon.

A *hon* under the Marathas usually consisted of 10 *takkas*, and a *takka* of 48 *rukas*. A *takka* was also equal to 6 annas of the pre-metric currency, and so an anna was equal to 8 *rukas*, and a paisa was equal to 2 *rukas*. Both these systems were prevalent in the Southern Maratha Country.

Money transactions: mortgage

Several sale and mortgage transactions took place in the Krishna-Tungabhadra Doab. For example on 27th October, 1586 Kalasappa of Bale-Hosur gave a sale deed for 30 *varahas* to Linganagauda of Mantur for the one-fourth part of the proceeds of his office of village accountant in the Bale-Hosur village.[1] On 4th May, 1679 Kenchangauda of Lakshmeshwar executed a mortgage-deed in favour of Virappa of Gadag mortgaging a land measuring 4½ *mars* from the *gaudikemanya* lands in Kadadi Kadamandi for a hundred *varahas*.[2] The *varahas* were sometimes mentioned as *gadyanas* as well. The 30 *varahas* paid by Mantur Lingana Gauda to Kalasappa, mentioned above, were called *priyasradimadhigadyana*.[3] There is another interesting case of mortgage of land being a part of the proceeds of an officer for 100 *varahas*. A certain Kenchana Gaudappa, son of Paruta Gauda belonging to Kadadi Honnapura Chenngauda and Chennakka, wife of Baramanagauda, both together mortgaged 4½ *mars* of land from the Kadadi Kadapatti-manya, being a part of their *gaudike-manya* to the creditor Suva Chennappa, the disciple of Marula Siddadeva of Saudi and to Boratayya Virappa of Gadag for 100 *varahas*. This land was given in mortgage in lieu of the payment of the yearly rent. But the *judi* or quit-rent due for this land was to be paid by the mortgagee himself. It was stipulated that the land was to be returned to the debtors when the loan would be repaid.[4] In another case a certain Govindaraya's son coming from Sirgaoppe Qasba in the Torgal sime mortgaged to Kenchanagauda of Lakshmeshwar half of his share of *gaudike* measuring 15 *mars* of land for 300 *sannagere varahas*.[5]

The denominations of the *varaha*, also called *gadyana* and *hon*, were the *bele, visa* and *kasu*. A *hon* was generally equivalent to four rupees, a *bele* equivalent to 8 annas (50 paise), a *visa* to 4 annas (25 paise) and a *kasu* to one anna (6 paise).

1. Bisma, LD 343.
2. *Ibid.*, LD 317.
3. *Ibid.*, LD 343.
4. *BISMA*, LD 318 dated 6-3-1679.
5. *Ibid.*, LD 24 dated 21-5-1654.

Mints

The Peshwas sought to organise mints in various places for coining sufficient amount of money for meeting the demands of trade and commerce.

After taking the fort of Dharwar in 1753 Nana Saheb Peshwa granted a *Kaulnama* dated 16th February, 1754 to the merchants and traders of Kasba Dharwad for establishing a new market to the east of the fort. The *Kaulnama* was addressed to the following persons:

Virat Sheti, Raddu Shetya, Shivalingappa Hubli, Ayanna Vahili, Basawalingappa Agadi, Kokana Annigeri, Venkanna Malakand Nirgar and Muddappa and to all the traders and shopkeepers. These merchants were asked to settle in the new market carrying on trade and commerce. They were exempted from the payment of land revenue for a period of seven years, after which the land revenue was to be levied according to the rates prevalent in the territories of Savanur Nawab.

Virat Shet was authorised to open a mint in the Peth for coining gold and silver coins, i.e. Hons and Rupees. No customs duties were to be levied on the commodities coming into the Peth for a year, after which they were to be levied at the rates prevalent in Savanur Nawab's territories.

An aftagir, a torch bearer, and a *chalavadi* (*i.e.* a servant of a Lingayat merchant carrying a large ladle with chain and bell on his shoulders) were allowed to these merchants. The merchants were required to build temples dedicated to Isvara and Hanumanta, and were assured that some land would be granted to them after the establishment of the Peth. They were allowed to build the Matha of Murgapaseti (*i.e.* Murga Math).

Visto Narayan was appointed Potdar of Peth, and the merchants were permitted to borrow Rs. 25,000 for the settlement of the Peth, the money to be repaid in a period of two years.

The merchants were further authorised to buy customs duties at the usual rates on the commodities passing that way except on cloth, elephants, horses, camels, cattle, and jewels on which the duties were to be levied at the rates current in Savanur Nawab's territories.

It is very interesting to note that they were also vested with the powers of administration of justice in their own locality. They were authorised to try the causes of the accused by forming the *Got*; if the *Got* was incapable of trying a particular case, it could be sent to the Central Government where justice would be done.[1]

---

1. *SSRPD*, II, 219, pp. 136-37.

In the Dharwad District Gazetteer it is mentioned that "owing to the dissensions between the commandant and the civil authorities in the town, the garrison were not allowed access to the petta and had much difficulty in getting privisions. The commandant represented the matter to the Peshwa, who ordered a new petta or the market to be built for the use of the garrison. It was built towards the north-east of the fort in 1753, and was called Sadashiv Peth, in honour of the Peshwa's cousin Sadashivrao, who had obtained the order for its building."[1]

In Dharwar and the neighbouring places a number of mints had been set up for coining Hons, Mohors and Rupees, but in due course the Jamindars proved dishonest and began to issue counterfeit coins resulting in considerable loss to the Maratha Government. Hence Nana Saheb Peshwa issued orders on 23rd October, 1760 to Pandurang Murar for abolishing all the mints in Subha Dharwad, establishing only one mint at Dharwad, and also for melting the counterfeit coins making them into the genuine ones.

For standardizing the mintage certain rules were laid down as follows:

1. The mould of the Hon must be as before.
2. The Ekeri Hon must be of 10 Kas and 3½ Masas in weight.
3. The Rupee must be genuine, and equal in weight to the Arcot Fulchari Rupee.
4. The Mohor must be of 12 Kas in weight like the Delhi Shikka Mohar.

For one year the dues to be paid to the Government by the Sawkars were remitted so as to allow the mints to earn some income. Therefore, according to the usual practice, 6 out of 1000 coins were to be collected for the Government. One Mohor coin per 1000 issued in addition to the above should be taken by Pandurang Murar himself.

Pandurang Murar was further instructed to keep with himself whatever seals of the Mohors and Rupees would be made. The perquisites of the artifices employed in the mint were to be given to them according to the usual practice.

5 Armed attendants were posted under Pandurang Murar. Their salary for one year was received from Narayanrao Venkatesh. Thereafter it was to be paid from the Government after the revenue settlement.

But the orders of Nana Saheb as regards the stoppage of all the mints in the Dharwad Subha and opening only one mint at Dharwad remained a dead letter with the result that Madhavrao also had to issue similar

1. *Gazetteer of the Bombay Presidency*, XXII, p. 672.

orders[1] in 1765 (31st August). In the same year on 20th September Madhavrao gave strict instructions as regards the minting and circulation of genuine coins to the following 11 Kamavisdars, to the Jamindars of 21 Parganas, Sawkars of 19 markets, artifices and assayers of 21 mints and to some other individuals.[2]

The following were the eleven Kamavisdars:

1. Narayanrao Venkatesh.
2. Visaji Narayan.
3. Anandrao Bhikaji.
4. Visaji Krishna.
5. Shesho Narayan.
6. Bhaskarrao Dadaji.
7. Giridharrao of the Savanur State.
8. Maloji Ghorpade.
9. Gopalrao Govind.
10. Yesaji Ram.
11. Other Kamavisadars and Thanedars.

The following were the Jamindars of the twenty-one parganas, *viz.* those of:

1. Gadak (Gadag)	2. Kittur	3. Hubli
4. Khanapur	5. Jamkhandi	6. Yadvad
7. Gokak	8. Nargund	9. Mudkavi
10. Manoli	11. Torgal (Sarkar)	12. Murgod
13. Chikodi	14. Ramdurg	15. Mudhol
16. Bagalkot	17. Vatkurki	18. Shahapur
19. Dharwad	20. Navalgund	21. Athani

The Sawakars were from the following nineteen markets or Peths:

1. Dharwad	2. Hubli	3. Betgeri
4. Navlagund	5. Nargund	6. Gadag
7. Lakshmeshwar	8. Gokak	9. Kittur
10. Yadvad	11. Bagalkot	12. Manoli Khanapur
13. Khanapur	14. Shahapur	15. Savanur
16. Haveri	17. Goa (port)	18. Koppal
19. Koppal		

1. *SSRPD*, VII, 718, pp. 291-93.
2. *Ibid.*, 719, pp. 293-97.

The artifices and the workers were from the following twenty-one places:

1. Manoli	2. Lakshmeshwar	3. Torgar
4. Athani	5. Shahapur	6. Gokak
7. Kittur	8. Yadwad	9. Murgod
10. Navalgund	11. Mudhol	12. Bagalkot
13. Jamkhandi	14. Batakurki	15. Mudakavi
16. Ramdurg	17. Nargund	18. Savanur
19. Bankapur	20. Dharwad	21. Chikodi

VI

Social Structure, Customs and Manners

The Southern Maratha Country was the meeting place of many castes and communities. In addition to the traditional castes one finds here a number of regional castes coming from other regions as well, and also a multiplicity of cartes based on occupations. Although the social structure is pyramidal with the Brahmin caste at the apex and the Shudra caste at the base, yet one finds many complexities in this structure, as the social stratification took place owing to the interaction of many forces such as the social status, the amount of wealth, and the administrative power that the members of the castes and classes possessed.

A lengthy Modi document from the Pune Archives[1], consisting of Kaifiyats, throw light on the various castes existing in the Southern Maratha Country during the Maratha period. The document gives details about a number of castes and sub-castes, their social and religious customs and manners. There are a number of references to these castes, sub-castes and also to Muslims in the earlier Modi documents as well, which corroborate the account given here. Hence these Kaifiyats give a fairly good and reliable account of the society of Maratha times in the Southern Maratha Country.

Among the Brahmins there were two main regional types, each consisting of 5 sub-types. The two main regional types were Pancha-Dravida and Pancha-Gauda. The Pancha-Dravida consisted of Andhra-Purva Desatha, Dravida Desastha, Karnataka Brahmins (this area was enclosed between the Tungabhadra in the north and the Kaveri in the south, in brief, the region lying to the south of the Southern Maratha

1. *Sannika*, 54, Part II.

Country), and finally the Desastha Brahmins living in the region between the Tungabhardra and the Bhima.

The Pancha-Gaudas could be Smartas, Vaishnavas or Bhagavats. They were Kanoji Brahmins, Kamarupi Brahmins, Utkala Brahmins, Maithili Brahmins and Gurjara Brahmins. Inter-marriage and interdining among these latter five were forbidden. They were strictly endogamous groups.

There were again the following 16 sub-castes among the Pancha-Dravids: Smarta, Kokanastha, Karhade, Varkari Madhyandin, Vanas, Karnatak, Shashtik, Nandavamshik, Srivaishnav Telang, Srivaishnava, Pratham-Shakhikanva, Kirvant, Sihavasai, Nurcher, Shenavi and Govalkonde. The Kokanasthas were also called Nutan Kokanastha Parashuram Shirish. These are said to have come from the sea shore in Kokan strip. These could be either Smarta or Bhagavat. They had the right to the performance of *Shatkarma*. Among these 16 sub-castes, 13 were *Shatkar-madhikaris*, while the remaining three were *Trikarmadhikaris*. These three sub-castes were Vanas, Sahavari and Shenavi. Earlier these had a right to the six karmas, but later on because of the commission of some improper act, they lost the right to the three karmas of dining (in others' houses), teaching, and acceptance of gifts, and retained the right to the remaining three karmas only.

The Brahmins celebrated the following festivals in a year:

1. *Yugadi on* Chaitra Shuddha 1
2. *Akshayya Tritiya* on Vaishakha Shuddha 3
3. *Nagara Panchami* on Shravana Shu. 5.
4. *Ganesh Chaturthi* on Bhadrapada Shu. 4.
5. *Navaratra*, from Ashvin Shu. 1 to 9.
6. *Vijaya Dashami* on Ashvin Shu. 10
7. *Dipavali*, from Ashvin Vadya 13 to Kartika Shu. 1 including Bal' Padva.
8. *Uththan Dvadashi* on Kartika Shu. 12
9. *Chhatti Navaratra* of Khandoba, from Margashirsha Shu. 1 to
10. *Simaga Paumima* on Phalguna Shu. 15
11. *Makara Sankrant* in the month of Paushya.
12. *Banashankari Navaratra*, from Paushya Shu. 8 to 15

In addition, they also observed 12 Paurnima days and 12 Ama' days as festivals. They were —

There were too many other festivals to be mentioned here.[1]

From the study of the contemporary Modi documents. We know that in this area mostly the following types of Brahmins lived and enjoyed a prestigious position in society. The Vaishnavas were of different types such as the followers of Madhvacharya, of Ramanujacharya, of Vallabhacharya, etc. But here the followers of Madhvacharya abounded. They were called Madhvas, and their names generally had the suffix of 'acharya'. Of course, even among the Shaivas there were some acharyas, but these were usually the heads of monasteries or other religious institutions. Otherwise the Shaivas had the suffix 'bhat' attached to their names. Anantacharya, Ramacharya, Vyasacharya, Keshavacharya, etc. may be given as the examples of Vaishnavas whereas Anantabhat, Ashvathbhat, Kasibhat, Krishnabhat, Guru-rayabhat were the Shaivas, also known as Smartas. Between the two, the Vaishnavas were, as a rule, more orthodox. Their names were Vaishnava names while the Shaivas could have Vaishnava names also. For example, the Vaishnavas would have only such names as Anantatirthacharya, Krishnacharya, Keshavacharya and the like, while that Sivas, besides having such Shaiva names as Nageshbhat, Mahadevbhat, etc., could also have Vaishnava names with the suffix 'bhat' like Govindbhat, Janardanbhat and Rambhat.[2] On the other hand, some common names like Appa, Gunda or Timma could be adopted by both the Vaishnavas and Shaivas.

There are a number of Modi documents[3] in the Pune Archives recording the grant of, or the continuation of the grant of, yearly allowances to the Brahmins. These documents give us an idea of the influence of the Brahmins in the society, their different branches, their movements in the Southern Maratha Country and also their service to the society. One such document is the *Jabta of Varshasanas* continued to Brahmins in Taluka Savanur which formed a major portion of the Southern Maratha Country. These Varshasanas or yearly allowances were continued to the Brahmins in 1792 which means that they must have been enjoying them for quite some time earlier.

These Brahmins were noted either for their scholarship and erudition or for their association with great religious orders, or for their cultural accomplishments. The allowances to Brahmins are arranged in the *Jabta* under 18 administrative divisions or Mahals including Parganas, Pethas or Qasbas. The document shows how the Peshwa Govt.

1. *Ibid.*
2. All the examples given here are taken from the original Modi documents.
3. KJ: 77 : 339; KJ: 324 : 4; KJ: 246 : 102, etc.

promoted social, cultural and religious progress of the people. It throws light on the movements of the Brahmin scholars and religious heads who became instrumental in the spread of culture and new ideas among the masses. These people going to several places, staying there for a certain length of time, meeting people, discussing with them various matters were indirectly educating the public.

The smallest amount of Varshasana given to an individual was of one *Chaval* (1/8 of a hon.), and the largest of Rs. 150.

Some of the recipients of Varsasanas were from outside the Southern Maratha Country, from such places as Bellary and Harapanahalli.

In the Southern Maratha Country there were a good number of Dikshits residing at various places such as Bankapur, Devgiri, Lakshmeshwar, Ramtirth, Adur, etc. Names like Ram Dikshit bin Mrityunjaya Diskhit, Vishwanath Dikshit, Narayana Dikshit, Vyenkata Dikshit, Ramapa Dikshit, Ram Dikshit bin Narayana Dikshit, Shiva Dikshit bin Sesha Dikshit, Ram Dikshit, Chandrasekhara Dikshit, Jagannath Dikshit, Virupaksha Dikshit, Tamana Dikshit Sugur, Subana Dikshit, Vishwanatha Dikshit, Devana Dikshit, Bawa Dikshit and Mani Dikshit probably suggest the continuance of the tradition of performing a number of complex religious rites and rituals especially connected with small sacrifices such as *homahavanas*, *griha-yajnas* and *vaishvadevas*.

The religious traditions in the Southern Maratha Country were continued by the Peshwa. The *Vyasa-puja* was performed as before three times in a year, *viz.*, on the days of *Kartika-purnima, Magha-purnima* and *Vaisakha-purnima*, and different sums were assigned for this *puja* in different Parganas. The highest sum, *viz.*, 33-12-0 rupees, was granted for this purpose from Hangal and Shiggaon Parganas. In Pargana Ranebennur 22-8-0 were granted while the lowest sum, 11-4-0, was paid from Airani and Adur Parganas. A number of religious orders prevalent in the country were the recipients of the Peshwa's Varsasanas. From Pargana Rattihalli the highest amount of Varsasana (18-12-0) was received by Sankarabharati Swami, the pontiff of the Sringeri Math, while the lowest amount (7-8-0) was received from Parganas Nidsangi and Tilavalli. Shri Satyabodh Swami, the pontiff of the Satyabodh Swami Math of Savanur, received Rs. 18-12-0 from Pargana Rattihalli; 9-6-0 from P/Hirekerur, 7-8-0 each from Parganas of Airani, Nidsangi and Tilavalli (in the last case specifically for *diparadhana*) and 5-10-0 from P/ Masur. The pontiff of the Kudalgi Math was the recipient of Rs. 11-4-0 from P/Kaginelli, 9-6-0 from P/Hirekerur, and 7-8-0 each from P/Airani and Kuppelur. Besides, the Math of Raghavendra Swami got Rs. 7-8-0 from P/Nidsangi and Bindacharya Swami of the Rangapur Math received Rs. 3-12-0 from P/Tilavalli for *diparadhana*. Subrahmanya Swami of Udupi was honoured in P/Kaginelli with a Varsasana of 52-8-0 rupees.

In addition to the religious orders and institutions a number of individuals got Varsasanas because of the religious or educational work that they were doing. Some individuals stand out prominent, and these generally got Varsasanas not from one Pargana only but in a number of Parganas, which shows the extent of their work, the field of their activity. An individual who was probably known for his erudition and proficiency in officiating at various ceremonies and rites, and who received the largest amount of Varsasana from the largest number of Parganas was Sankara Bhat of Misrikot. He received Rs. 67-8-0 in all from 8 Parganas out of 16. He got Rs. 18-12-0 from P/Hangal, 7-8-0 each from P/Kod, Tilavalli, Airani, Chikkerur, Ranebennur and Kaginelli, while from P/Halgeri 3-12-0 only were received. Another individual of Misrikot who was well known was Anayacharya. Umapati Sastri from Harihar was a great scholar who received Varsasanas from P/Ranebennur, P/Airani, P/Masur and P/Kod. He was probably an Aradhya Saiva. The Upadhyes and Adhyapaks imparted education to the pupils in the traditional way. Grants of lands and cash were generally made to such teachers for carrying on their work of teaching and spreading education among the public. One such Upadhye was Gururaya Bhat of Bankapur who was paid Varsasana from P/Chikkerur, P/Airani, P/Hirekerur, P/Tilavalli and P/Kod. Others included Ramacharya Upadhye of Bankapur and Sivabhat Adhyapak of Misrikot.

Masur had the privilege of offering two reputed scholars from the family of Pandurangi, *viz.*, Balacharya and Ramacharya. They were honoured with Varsasanas in Peth Haveri, in Ps/Hirekerur, Kaginelli, Kuppelur, Shiggaon, Rattihalli, and, of course, Masur, ranging from 7-8-0 rupees in p/Haveri to 56-4-0 in P/Masur. Three other members surnamed Pandurangi, who were not much known, were Timanachari, Srinivasachari and Anachari. Hirekerur produced a great scholar in the person of Vyenkata Sastri to whom the Varasasanas flowed from Ps/Hangal, Tilavalli, Airani, Kerur Khurd, Kerur Budruk and Kod. Narayana Dikshit was another name associated with Hirekerur. Jairam Sastri was a famous pandit from Savanur, and his erudition was much honoured in Ps/Rattihalli, Adur, Kaginelli, Hangal, Peth Haveri and Qasba Halgeri. Narayana Dikshit of Devagiri (Devaragudda) was another reputed scholar (to whom a reference has already been made above) who was evidently known for his proficiency in officiating at sacrifices and other rituals. He received Varsasanas from Ps/Kaginelli, Ranebennur, Kerur Khurd, Nidsangi, Kod, Hangal and Qasba Halgeri. From Savanur came a Brahmin called Anayacharya Navaratne whose ancestors were probably honoured with nine varieties of gems for their erudition. Hence the name of Navaratne was retained by their family. Anayacharya was greatly honoured in Ps/Ranebennur, Adur, Kuppelur and Peth Haveri. Other less known members of this family seem to have been Mudgalacharya, Krishnacharya, and Apayacharya. It appears that the religious tradition of worshippng fire by keeping it burning all the 24 hours was still continued by a few Brahmins in the Savanur principality. Such were Balambhat Agnihotri of Rattihalli and Savanur, Siva Dikshit Agnihotri of Bankapur, and Timana Dikshit Agnihotri of Hangal.

About the *Kshatriyas* also the document (*Sannika*, 54) gives some details. For example, the ideal period for thread ceremony for them was between the 8th and 16th year of the boy. Brahma, Deva, Arsha, Gandharva, Rakshasa and Paishachya — these 6 types of marriage were permitted for them. But they did not follow these rules during the Peshwa and Company periods. Among the *Shatkarmas Yajana*, *adhyayana* and *dana*, these three Karmas they could perform. But they had no right to the other three karmas, *viz*., yajana, adhyapana, and pratigraha.

During the Maratha period, however, there were very few such Kshatriyas in the Southern Maratha Country. Their number was negligible.

The *Vaishyas* were known as *Komatis*. Unlike the Kshatriyas, they did not have a right to the three Karmas. They had a right only to the karma of *dana*, while they had no right to *yajana* and *adhyayana*. They worshipped the god Nagareshwar and the goddess Bavani Kanika. These were their caste deities and they could also have their over favourite gods, or *ishta-devatas*. They had the *Brahmin guru* or priest.

The Jains constituted a major portion of society in the Southern Maratha Country. The *Jatakarma* was performed as soon as the child was born, the naming ceremony was performed on the 13th day, the hair-cutting ceremony in 3 years, and the tuft of hair (*shendi*) was left in the 5th year after performing an appropriate ceremony. The boy was sent to school in the 5th/8th/9th year, and the thread ceremony was performed before the 7th/9th/10th year. Thereafter the marriage could be celebrated any time.

Evening meals were to be taken before sunset. While taking meals the Jain should not hear about others except the people of his own house, hence a bell was rung during the meals. They cremated their dead. There was no remarriage among the Jains.

These people celebrated the festivals of Yugadi, Nagpanchami, Navaratra, Dasara, Dipavali and Anarit Paurnima. They put on the sacred thread on Shravana Paurnima. Like the Brahmins, they celebrated all the remaining Paurnimas and Amavasyas.

The Jains were supposed to engage themselves in trade and commerce. They were forbidden to indulge in violence. The document says that their god was Lord Buddha. [Here he should have been Lord Mahavira. Probably the man who gave the Kaifiyat did not know Mahavira.]

The *Shudra* was also called *Kuda* or *Kaligo*. He had to undergo only the Puranokta Samskaras. As per the book "Shuddha-Kamalakara", they performed Samskaras, *viz.*, Garbhadana, Pumsavana, Avalokana, Simanta, Jatakarma, Namakarana, Annaprashana, Chaulakarma, Chhurika-bandhana, Munja, Vivaha and Antyakarma. The girl had to marry before puberty. There was no remarriage for her. The Shudra was supposed to serve the cows, Brahmins, etc. Some of them embraced Lingayatism and were observing the rules and regulations of the Lingayat sect.

Among the *Lingayats* the reception of the Linga by means of initiation had great significance. It was so important that even a three-month baby in the womb of its mother was supposed to receive the Linga. But the actual Linga was tied to the mother until the birth of the baby. After its birth the baby was made to receive the Linga in the following way. Soon after the birth of the child, the Linga was tied to it. After washing the feet of the Guru that water was put into its mouth. Then its mother's milk mixed with honey was given to the baby to drink. Among the many practices this was the best one. The Linga could also be tied on the 5th or 13th day.

The initiation was given by the Guru, the Panchacharyas and their gods together. The ritual followed here was as follows: First, the boy to be initiated should have a complete shave. Then he should take bath in a river or with river water or with any water feeling that it was river water. Then before entering the house he should take bath first with the cow-urine and then again with water. Next the *Durva* water should be poured on him five times from head to foot. He should then roll three times on a cloth spread on the ground. He should then again take a bath, apply ashes of cow-dung to his body, take in his hands *Darbha* grass, fruits, some gold, flowers and new clothes, and stand outside the house. On consulting the people and the Guru inside, he should be called inside and made to prostrate himself before the Guru. Then the five holy pots should be kept as follows: the pot of Revana Siddheshwar in the east, that of Ekorama Deva in the south, that of Marula Siddheshwar in the west, that of Panditaradhya in the north, and that of Panchevanagi Siddhanijeshwar in the fifth. Placing fruits on these five pots, covering them with new cloth the Mathapati should worship them. Then the Jangam, worshipping the Linga should place it on his *Gadagi* or throne spreading some rice on it. Next he takes up the Linga, covers it up in a piece of cloth, and ties it round the neck of the boy.

Finally the boy was made to take the holy water with which the Guru's feet were washed, and also the puffed rice as *prasad*. For tying the linga to anybody, this ritual of initiation had to be undergone

The boys should marry between 12 and 25 years of age; if it was not possible, they were permitted to marry upto the age of 36. For the girls the best period for marriage was between the 5th and 7th years; if not, upto the 11th year, and if this also was not possible, then finally as a last resort upto the 12th year. In any case she should marry before puberty. Divorce and widow marriage were allowed. They celebrated festivals during the whole months of Kartik and Shravan, and in the rest of the ten months on three days every week, namely, Monday, Tuesday, and Thursday Similarly 10 Paurnimas and 10 Amavasyas, Shivaratri, Yugadi, Dasara, Dipavali and Simaga Paurnima were celebrated by them as festivals.

The Lingayats buried their dead. Many details are given about the procedure or ritual of burying the dead in the documents. As they are matters of detail, they are not given here.

To all those members of other castes who embraced Lingayatism the chief deity was Ishwar, the *ishta-devalas* were Venkoba, Yellamma etc., and the Guru was the Jangama.

There were a large number of Lingayats in this area. They were found as Desais, Nadgaudas, administrative officers and great landholders, and many of them who came from the lower strata of society and embraced Lingayatism retained their earlier positions in society, now having greater social status. All these were knit in an organisation whose rules and regulations were governed by the Jangamas and by innumerable *mathas*. It may be noticed that the Peshwas do not seem to have supported the Lingayat Mathas, although the Brahmin Mathas such as the Sringeri

Country), and finally the Desastha Brahmins living in the region between the Tungabhardra and the Bhima.

The Pancha-Gaudas could be Smartas, Vaishnavas or Bhagavats. They were Kanoji Brahmins, Kamarupi Brahmins, Utkala Brahmins, Maithili Brahmins and Gurjara Brahmins. Inter-marriage and interdining among these latter five were forbidden. They were strictly endogamous groups.

There were again the following 16 sub-castes among the Pancha-Dravids: Smarta, Kokanastha, Karhade, Varkari Madhyandin, Vanas, Karnatak, Shashtik, Nandavamshik, Srivaishnav Telang, Srivaishnava, Pratham-Shakhikanva, Kirvant, Sihavasai, Nurcher, Shenavi and Govalkonde. The Kokanasthas were also called Nutan Kokanastha Parashuram Shirish. These are said to have come from the sea shore in Kokan strip. These could be either Smarta or Bhagavat. They had the right to the performance of *Shatkarma*. Among these 16 sub-castes, 13 were *Shatkar-madhikaris*, while the remaining three were *Trikarmadhikaris*. These three sub-castes were Vanas, Sahavari and Shenavi. Earlier these had a right to the six karmas, but later on because of the commission of some improper act, they lost the right to the three karmas of dining (in others' houses), teaching, and acceptance of gifts, and retained the right to the remaining three karmas only.

The Brahmins celebrated the following festivals in a year:

1. *Yugadi on* Chaitra Shuddha 1
2. *Akshayya Tritiya* on Vaishakha Shuddha 3
3. *Nagara Panchami* on Shravana Shu. 5.
4. *Ganesh Chaturthi* on Bhadrapada Shu. 4.
5. *Navaratra*, from Ashvin Shu. 1 to 9.
6. *Vijaya Dashami* on Ashvin Shu. 10
7. *Dipavali*, from Ashvin Vadya 13 to Kartika Shu. 1 including Bali Padva.
8. *Uththan Dvadashi* on Kartika Shu. 12
9. *Chhatti Navaratra* of Khandoba, from Margashirsha Shu. 1 to 6.
10. *Simaga Paumima* on Phalguna Shu. 15
11. *Makara Sankrant* in the month of Paushya.
12. *Banashankari Navaratra*, from Paushya Shu. 8 to 15

In addition, they also observed 12 Paurnima days and 12 Amavasya days as festivals. They were —

Puarnimas

1. Chaitrya: Havanada Hunvi
2. Vaishakha: Agi Hunvi
3. Jeshtha: Kar Hunvi
4. Ashadha: Kadalgadabina Hunvi
5. Shravana: Nul Hunvi
6. Bhadrapada: Anantana Hunvi
7. Kartika: Gauri Hunvi
8. Margashirsha: Hostala Hunvi
9. Pushya: Banada Hunvi
10. Magha: Bharat Hunvi
11. Phalgun: Holi Hunvi

(In this list Ashvin is missing)

Amavasyas

1. Karagada Amasi
2. Badami Amasi
3. Manyettina Amasi
4. Kadabole Amasi
5. Divasi Amasi
6. Divagi Amasi
7. Chhetti Amasi
8. Yel Amasi
9. Avaratana Amasi
10. Sivaram Amasi
11. Ugadi Amasi

(Here again Ashvin seems to be missing)

Besides these, there were some other festivals which the Brahmins were supposed to observe. They were —

1. *Davana Chavati* on Shravan Shu. 4
2. *Ananta Chaturdashi* on Bhadra, Shu. 14
3. Rathasaptami on Magha Shu. 7
4. Bhagini Tritiya on Kartika Shu. 3
5. Bhavabidigi on Kartika Shu. 2

Math, the Satyabodh Math, and the Kudali Math were the recipients of their grants. However, they are found remitting the judi tax on the temples of Basavanna-Deva. Virabhadra-Deva and Shankaralinga-Deva[1] which might have been built by the Lingayats. On the other hand we find a tax on the Jangamas called *ganachari*.[2]

The document says that the life of the Marathas and that of the Vaishyas were governed by similar rules. Their Samskaras were governed as per the book, *Shudra Kamalakara*. This seems to be wrong. On the other hand the Marathas were closer to the Kshatriyas. The Samskaras in their life were *Prasta, Simanta, Jatakartna, Namakarana, Chaula, Shendi, Munja, Lagna* and *Phalashobhana*. The girl had to marry before puberty. They cremated their dead. There was no remarriage among them

Some of their customs were like those of Kshatriyas, especially in respect of marriages and division of ancestral property. In other words, their life was governed by the rules of both Kshatriyas and Vaishyas. Kings and Sardars were strict about these rules, while ordinary Marathas, poor Marathas living in villages or rural areas were not very particular about these rules. Remarriages did take place among such rural Maratha folk, although the rule was against it.

The Marathas along with Brahmins and in very few cases Lingayat Desais wielded great power and influence in the Southern Maratha Country. We find them occupying positions of power and prestige in the administrative set-up. And these Brahmin and Maratha administrative officers got a sizable amount of revenue from the lands in the village by way of *dumala* and *mokasa* dues. The revenue documents, especially *Dehzadas, Yadis* and sometimes even *Talebands* are replete with the names of such administrative officers, and also of the Brahmin, Maratha and a few Lingayat Zamindars who seized the revenue of the lands from the rayats without contributing anything to the cultivation of lands. This was largely due to the attitude of the Brahmin Peshwas, who in league with the Marathas, were trying to maintain their sway in the Country. Some examples are given below.

A document[3] of 1796 gives the names of various Brahmin and Maratha revenue officials who were in charge of the collection of revenue from different parganas as shown below:

1. KJ: 241 : 355.
2. KJ: 354.
3. KJ: 243.

Pargana	**Officials**
Kaginelli	1. Pandurang Bhaskar Kamavisdar
	2. Ramchandra Narayan Daptardar
	3. Visaji Raghunath Sabnis.
Kod	1. Kamavisdars (two)
	(a) Ramchandra Govind (for *Ihide* and *Isanne*)
	(b) Yesaji Govind (*Salas* onwards)
	2. Ganesh Narasi Phadnis
	3. Ganesh Narasi Daptardar
Kuppelur	1. Venkatrao Sivaji Kamavisadar
	2. Moro Gopal Phadnis
Shiggaon	1. Appaji Govind Kamavisdar
	2. Keso Narayan Daptardar
Nidsangi	1. Sivaji Khanderao Kamavisdar
	2. Kasi Vithal Phadnis
	3. Ganesh Jagannath Daptardar
	4. Naraso Baburao Sabnis
Tilvalli	1. Govind Bapuji Phadnis
Adur	1. Sadashiv Ramachandra Phadnis
	2. Bapuji Raoji Sabnis
Rattihalli	1. Devrao Anant Kamavisdar
	2. Naro Mahadev Phadnis
	3. Daji Moreshwar Daptardar
Guttal	1. Narayan Bhaskar Kamavisdar
Okh	1. Lingo Baburao Kamavisdar
	2. Yado Bhikaji Phadnis
	3. Pandurang Mahadev Sabnis
Hangal	1. Trimbakrao Ballal Kamavisdar
	2. Dhondo Bhaskar Phadnis
	3. Ramchandra Krishna Sabnis
Masur	1. Raghunath Baburao Kamavisdar
	2. Dado Krishna Phadnis
	3. Shankaraji Krishna Daptardar

Morab	1. Anandrao Ramchandra Kamavisdar
	2. Hari Narayan Phadnis
	3. Krishnaji Narayan Daptardar
Karadgi	1. Subarao Anant Kamavisdar
Qasba	1. Appaji Devrao Kamavisdar
Havasbhavi	
Qasba	1. Chinto Anant Kamavisdar
Kerur Khurd	2. Nanaji Venkatesh C/o Sadashiv Mahadev Phadnis
	3. Vasudev Gopal Daptardar
Karyat Annigeri	1. Janardan Bachyaji Phadnis
Desgat	1. Raghunath Bhaskar Kamavisdar
	2. Jivaji Keshav Phadnis
	3. Shesho Narhar Sabnis
	4. Sakho Ramchandrao Daptardar

Zakat Taluka Savanur under Vinayak Raghunath Khare.

In the second example[1] we get the details of the villages enjoyed by the Inamdars and the villages assigned in *dumala* and the *khalsa* lands together with the land revenue they yielded in the Savanur Taluka which formed, as said earlier, a large portion of the Southern Maratha Country.

There were 14 Parganas, 2 Qasbas and 1 Peth in Taluka Savanur in 1793 as shown below:

Parganas	**Villages**	**Alienated + Khalsa**
1. Adur	71	(9 + 62)
2. Hangal	68	(24 + 44)
3. Shiggaon	21	(3 + 18)
4. Ranebennur	66	(16 + 50)
5. Nidsangi	64	(13 + 51)
6. Tilavalli	37	(11 + 26)
7. Rattihalli	44	(20 + 24)
8. Kerur Khurd	16	(3 + 13)
9. Kuppelur	43	(2 + 38 + 3 attached
10. Guttal	48	(7.50 + 4.50)
11. Kod	40	(5 + 35)

1. KJ: 246.

12.	Airani	18	(1 + 17)
13.	Kaginelli	86	(7 + 78 + 1 Mahal Petha)
14.	Masur	16	(nil + 16)
	Qasbas		
1.	Havasbhavi		
2.	Halgeri		
	Peth		
1.	Peth Haveri		

Among the 71 villages in Pargana Adur 6 were of Inamdars, 3 were *dumala* and 62 *khalsa*. Of the Inamdars Gurarao Narasimha had the *mukasa* of 2 villages, and Nadgauda Havanurkar Desai enjoyed the revenue of 2 villages. In Pargana Hangal 21 were alienated villages and 44 Khalsa villages. Among the alienated villages, 7 were Desai-mukasa villages enjoyed by Govind Narasimh and Srinivas Venkaji, another 7 were *Deshpande-mukasa* villages enjoyed by Rudro Kalo and Mahado Bishne. One was with Bijumal Desai and Deshpande, 5 were with Nadgauda Havnurkar, 1 with Basappa Pattanasetti of Mauje Galehalli, 3 were *dumala*, one being enjoyed by the pontiff of Sringeri, and two by Syed Nasir-ud-din Pirjade. In Pargana Shiggaon 5 were inam villages, of which 2 were with Srinvas Trimal Deshpande Nadgauda and 1 with Kille Bankapur, and the remaining 18 were *Khalsa*. In Pargana Ranebennur 5 were under Tipu lying beyond the Tungabhadra. They were, however, iven in *inam* to the Sringeri pontiff. Five were with the Zamindar Desai ınmantgauda Havnurkar and 1 with the Zamindar Nadgir. Two were h the pontiffs of the *mathas*, one with the Sringeri pontiff and the r with Satyabodh Swami.

ı Pargana Nidsangi 3 villages had gone to Taluka Bankapur and 2 ka Swadi. Six were with the Zamindars: 1 was with Gurumallappa with Ramaji Bhimaji Desai, 2 with Deshpande Samat and 1 with ıdo and Girmaji Dado Deshpande. Pargana Tilavalli consisted villages, 2 *devadaya* villages and 1 *mathamanya* village. Four es were with Desai Hanmantgauda Havnurkar and 4 with hivrao Kalo and Bhimaji Mahadev. One village was granted es of the temple of Sri Hanmantadeva of Satenahalli and was for the services of the god Hanmant of Chaksinkop. uddadamallapur was for Sriguru Satyabodh Swami of na Rattihalli there were 5 *inam* villages, 2 for Satyabodh ch for Sringeri Swami, Sri Raghavendra Swami and Sri

Krishna Deva of Udupi. One village was with the enemy in Taluka Harihar for the last 20 years. Fourteen villages were with Havnurkar Desai. The remaining 24 were *Khalsa.* In Kerur Khurd 3 were alienated and 13 were Khalsa. Of the alienated, 1 was under Udugani Mahal in Taluka Bidnur, and 2 were granted in inam, one as *sarvatnnya* to Hanmantgauda Desai Havnurkar and the other as *manya* to Timapa Gurarao Nadgir. In Pargana Kuppelur there were 2 *inam* villages, one for Sri Satyabodh Swami and the other for Sri Sankarabharati of Kudali Sangam Math. Thirty-eight were *Khalsa*, and the remaining 3 were under attachment. These were formerly with Devanabhat Bhanbhat Joshi, Harbhat Ayambhat Joshi and Nadgir of Rattihalli and Kuppelur as *inam* villages.

In Pargana Guttal 5 villages were granted in *inam* to Hanmantagauda Havnurkar Desai, and 2½ to the Brahmins. Of these one was with Vishnappa Rangapurkar, another with Somayaji of Harpanahalli, and a half village was with Seshbhat Puranik Havnurkar. The rest were *Khalsa* In Pargana Kod 5 were alienated, of which 4 were with the Zamindar Hanmantagauda Desai and 1 with the Zamindar Nadgir, the rest were *khalsa.* In Pargana Airani 1 village was with Hanmantagauda Desai Havnurkar, the rest being *khalsa.* In Pargana Kaginelli 7 were *inam* villages, 6 with Hanmantagauda Desai Havnurkar and 1 for the services in the temple of Sri Adikeshavadeva of Kaginelli. This was a judi village. Qasba Haveri was a Peth Mahal and the remaining 78 were *khalsa.*

Bapuji Shinde, a Maratha, was the Killedar of Dharwad fort in 1794 A.D.[1] Siddoji Naik Nimbalkar enjoyed the saranjams of Karyat Annigeri in 1811 A.D.[2] He was also in possession of the village of Haripali in Taluka Manoli.[3] Similarly in 1773 the village of Apsinge in Taluka Chikodi was with Janoji Nimbalkar as a dumalegaon.[4]

There were no hard and fast rules for the Redars,[5] who formed the next caste. There was no fixed *karma* for the Redar from his birth to his marriage. He could marry any time. 'The girl had to marry preferably before puberty, but could do so even afterwards. Remarriage was permissible. Quite a number of them had embraced Lingayatism.

The Redars' Guru Acharya was at Tirupati and Kanakagiri. They took the *mudra* and tirtha (holy water). The *mudra* was a seal of the

1. KJ: 49 : 206.
2. KJ: 246 : 102
3. *Ibid.*
4. KJ: 349 : 289.
5. The Redar caste should not be confused with the Bedar caste. The Redar was a separate caste having its own identity.

symbol of their sect, and this seal or *mudra* was, after heating it, pressed on some part of the body so that the symbol of their sect remained on their body. This was known as *Nama-dharana*. The *Namadharis* were Vaishnavas. Of course, those who became Lingayats followed the rules of Lingayat cult. Interdining and intermarriage were allowed between such Lingayats and Redars.

Their marriage ceremony used to last for four days. On the first day the worship of rice called *Akki-puja* was performed. The procedure of this puja was as follows: People from the side of the bridegroom brought one *kudo* or 5 *payalis* of rice and 16 *payalis* of gram to the house of the bride, there they worshipped the rice and gram and fed the members of their caste, and applied turmeric powder to boys and girls. On the second day the worship of the gods was conducted. On the third day the actual marriage was celebrated, and finally on the last day the marriage procession was taken out, which was followed by *Nagoli* and *Ghar-Bharani*. To consummate the whole marriage ceremony the members of the caste attending the marriage were sumptuously fed.

They celebrated the festivals of Yugadi, Navaratri, Dasara, Dipavali, Nagapanchami, Shivaratri, Gokulashtami and Anantachaturdashi. They also celebrated every Monday in the months of Shravana and Kartika as well as 12 Paurnimas and 12 Amavasyas and every Dvadashi after fasting on every Ekadashi. Those that had become Lingayats also celebrated these festivals except Ekadashi, Gokulashtami and Anantachaturdashi. The Namadharis cremated their dead, while those that had become Lingayats buried their dead.

Namdhari Redars had Venkoba as their tutelary god, Shri Vaishnava Acharya as their priest and to the Lingayat converts, besides the above god, Ishvara was their *ishta-devata* and the Jangam was their priest. The Redars also played an important part in the political and administrative life of the country.

Koshti or *Halkar* was another caste. Their family deities were Bana-Shankari and Ishwar and the priest was Devagayya who resided in his Math at Hampi. On the 5th day after the birth of the child a function called the *Iral* ceremony was performed. The *jaival, shendi, munj, lagna* and *shobhana* — these Samskaras were performed. Divorce and widow remarriage were permissible.

The marriage ceremony was performed under the guidance of their priest Devagayya or the village Joshi. The practice of paying *teravu* was in vogue. The usual festivals were celebrated, such as Yugadi, Dipavali and

Bana-Shankari Navaratra. The dead were usually cremated. The Koshtis were an endogamous group. If any member of the caste eloped with a girl from another caste or took flesh and wine, he was excommunicated. After the payment of a penalty ranging from Rs. 10 to Rs. 50 or depending upon the ability of the person to pay, he or she was made to undergo the purificatory rituals and then taken back into the caste. Of the penalty amount, half went to the Government, and the other half to Devagayya. The division of the ancestral property was done as per the custom prevalent in the Redar caste.

The cobblers (Hajam) formed the next caste. Originally they were Hindus. Later some of them accepted Lingayatism, and then under the Muslim rule some were converted to Islam. Similarly the *Kasais* or butchers by caste were formely Hindus, but during the reign of Aurangzeb many of them embraced Islam.

Dalal was another caste. Its members were the devotees of Hindu gods such as Hanuman. They had no regular priest, some of the caste-members themselves accepting the responsibilities of a preist. Divorce and widow remarriage were allowed. The *teravu* was Rs. 8 for the marriage and Rs. 7 for the remarriage. They dined only with the Lingayats, and not with the members of the other castes. Their occupation was working in wool. Their customs and manners were usually like those of Shudras. They cremated their dead, if they were Namadharis, others were buried. The division of property and the celebration of festivals were done as per the custom of the land.

The members of the *Padmasali* caste performed the customs regarding the Javal, Shendi, Munj, Lagna, Shobana and Namakarana in respect of their boys. They cremated their dead. They also performed the *paksha* ritual in the *Paksha* month. They were the devotees of Venkoba and Lakshmi and their Guru was Shrivaishnava Acharya. These tilled the lands and did other sundry jobs. Otherwise they begged assuming the role of the *Dasaris*.

Among the Hindus anybody could become a *Dasari*. He worshipped Venkoba and Lakshmi and his Guru was Shrivaishnava Acharya, who was a Brahmin. The rest were living according to the practices of the *Padmasali* caste members.

Banagars had embraced Lingayatism. So their god was Virabhadradeva and the Jangam was their priest. They spun white threads and dyed the cloth red. They also stitched blouses (*choli*). They were experts in this work. They were also engaged in agriculture and trade. Divorce and widow remarriage were allowed. At marriages and remarriages (*udaki* — a Kannada word) the *teravu* was paid ranging from 5 *hons* to 12 *hons*. *Teravu* was a Kannada word and meant bride price, that is, the money paid by the bridegroom's family to the bride's family. It is the opposite of dowry. The rest of the customs and manners followed the Lingayat rules.

The *Gollars* or cowherds were members of the Gollar caste. Their tutelary god was Krishnadeva Venkoba and the Guru was Shrivaishnava Acharya also known as Namadhari Kankagirikar.

The marriage was celebrated for four days. On the first day they had what was known as *Bhuma*. On that day nine married women were invited to the meals at the *Bhuma*. For the *Bhuma* 5 quarter-sers of rice, 5 quarter-sers of wheat and 5 sers of jaggery were taken and made into sweet chapatis (*poli*). These were served along with 5 sers of milk at the *Bhuma*. This dish the husband and wife had to eat along with the above 9 married women. If something was left the Devawale could eat. But the members of other castes were forbidden even to see it, much less to eat it.

On the second day the worship of the betelnuts called *Adki Puja* was performed. Two mounds of unbroken betelnuts were brought to the holy chamber of God in the house. Then the God's chamber was cleaned, and thick iron rod (*batta*) was kept there, and was worshipped. Then on the raised platform in a cleaned place a blanket was spread, incense was burnt, the rod was placed, and over this betelnuts were poured. This the husband and wife worshipped and to this they offered food offerings. All this was conducted in the presence of Kattimaniwale.

The distribution of betelnuts was to be done as follows: A bowl containing nine betelnuts, 5 put by the boy and 4 by the girl, was taken as a measure. Such 5 bowls of betelnuts were given to the Government, 5 to the Desai, 5 to the Patil, 5 to the Kulkarni, 5 to the Deshpande and ½ to the Barabalute (*i.e.*, 12 village servants). Thereafter the remaining betelnuts were distributed among the caste-members giving 10 or 8 or 5 or 4 or 3 or 2 or 1 to each one of them depending upon their number. But before the actual distribution took place, 4 honourable ladies again offered offerings to the married women after the worship, and then the distribution of the betelnuts was done.

On the third day the ritual of *Nagavali Gharbharani* was performed, and finally after one more ceremony the marriage came to be completely consummated.

The festivals were celebrated by the Gollars as per the custom of the land. However, among these festivals the festival of *Gokulashtami* was most important, because they belonged to the Yadava clan, in which Lord Krishna had been born.

The *Telang Banajewars* worshipped Venkoba and their priest was Kankagirikar Shrivaishnava Acharya. For performing marriage ceremony etc. they used to have a Brahmin Purohit. They cremated their dead. The rules regarding excommunication, purification and the reception of the mudra were similar to those of Gollars. The division of ancestral property etc. was done according to the custom of the country. The festivals were celebrated like the Hindus. The *teravu* of 5 hons each was taken for the marriage and remarriage. Taking wine and flesh was forbidden as in many other castes.

In regard to the *Mushtiger* caste, it may be noted that their god and priest were similar to those of Telang Banajewars. The *teravu* for the marriage was 32 rupees, the details of which were as in the Redar caste. Rs. 30 to 40 were taken for the remarriage.

Many of these caste-members had become Lingayats, and many others had put on the sacred thread becoming Desais and others. The Desais and others became Jamidars. There was no remarriage among them, among others it was allowed. Their festivals were like those of the rest of the Hindus.

The *Telis* or the oilmen had accepted Lingayatism. Karekulada Ganigers and Sajan Ganigers constituted two of its sub-divisions. The members of the first were many in number. Interdining between the two was allowed, but not intermarriage. Among the Sajan Ganigers there was no re-marriage. But it was allowed among other Telis. The *teravu* of 5 hons for the marriage and 12 hons for the remarriage was taken. Other customs were more or less like those of the Lingayats.

The members of the *Jir* caste, also known as *Garavis*, were usually the Lingayats. They were shepherds' priests. Their conduct was governed by the Lingayat rules and regulations. Those who had not accepted Lingayatism lived like Kunabis. To these the god was Mahadev, and the priest was Jangam. The marriage *teravu* was 10 *hons*. They buried their dead. Their hereditary occupation was to act as *devapujaris*, that is, to supply the various articles necessary for the worship of the god, to provide flowers and holy leaves etc., to stitch the broad leaves into pans or plates on which to serve the food, and in some places to make public announcements by beating drums.

The deities of the *Dhanagars* or shepherds were Birappa, Mailar Linga and Khandoba, Honakari Deva, Hanamappa and Yellamma, while the priest was one among his caste-members. The Brahmins officiated at the marriages. Rs. 10/- for the marriage and Rs. 20/- for the remarriage were taken as the *teravu.* Later the amount increased. Vriddhi-Kshaya rules were observed as per the customs of the land. They both buried and cremated their dead. Taking *sindi* (local liquor) and *sharab* (wine) was forbidden. If this rule was violated by anybody, he was excommunicated.

Hande Kurabi was another caste. Many of them had accepted Lingayatism. The division of ancestral property and the celebration of festivals were done as per the custom of the country. Big Sardars like Holkars belonged to such a caste only. The *Goravs* constituted a sub-caste of the Hande Kurabi caste.

The *Panchala* caste is supposed to be a composite caste comprising five artisan sub-castes, namely, the goldsmith, the blacksmith, the brass-smith, the carpenter and the mason. Thus the word Panchala denotes these five artisan castes collectively. Usually they are exogamous groups. In some cases, the word denotes a composite caste of the following artisan sub-castes, namely, the carpenter, the weaver, the barber, the washerman and the shoemaker. Here the smithy castes are missing, and these are of a lower category than the earlier ones. But generally, the practice regarding the number of the constituent sub-castes is not strictly adhered to. The word Panchala could be used even for more than 5 constituent castes which may include other lower castes than the ones mentioned above. And in our documents here, this is the case. Here the *Panchal* caste was a composite caste consisting of 7 artisan castes, namely, the *Sonar* (goldsmith), *Lohar* (blacksmith), *Sutar* (carpenter), *Kumbhar* (potter), *Bhandi-Karanar* (maker of vessels), *Kasar* (maker of glass bangles), and *Kalla-Kutkar* (stone-cutter). The document says that there were in all 5 castes in the Panchal composite caste, although it enumerates 7 castes actually. Interdining was allowed. The priest was their own caste-man, and later the caste-man was Dharmada-Aiya or a religious mendicant. Their god was Sirasangi Kalawwa in the Navalgunda Taluka. The Samaskaras from birth to death were on the whole like those of the land Their priest or the Joshi of the village officiated at the marriage and other ceremonies. They did not apply ashes to the forehead, but applied sandal paste.

The *Jalagar* was strictly an occupational caste The other caste people such as Marathas, Musalmans, Kabirs, etc., many times accepted the Jalagar occupation, but followed their own caste rules in their conduct.

The *Kallakutaka* occupation was also followed by the Muslims, and of course by *Vadars*. The family gods of Vadars were Venkoba and

Hanamantadev, and the priest was Shrivaishnava Acharya. Divorce and widow remarriage were practised among them. They buried their dead. If he was a Dasari and a Mudra-bearer, he was cremated. The Vadars lived outside the village in huts, except a few who lived in the houses. But the latter practice was limited.

The traditional sub-division of the Vadar or Vodda caste was into three endogamous groups, namely, Kallu Voddas, Mannu Voddas and Uppu Voddas. 'Kallu' in Kannada means stone, hence their occupation was excavation of stone from quarries, stone-cutting and allied pursuits 'Mannu' in Kannada means earth, hence these Voddas were working in earth and allied pursuits. And 'Uppu' in Kannada means, as pointed out in connection with the caste of Uppars, salt, hence these Voddas engaged themselves in pursuits connected with salt. Some of their functions might have been similar to those of Uppars.

However, here the Kaifiyat gives a slightly different but more detailed account of the sub-divisions of the Vaddar or Vodda caste. It has wisely dropped the Uppu Voddas whose functions the Uppars were performing. The document says that among the Vadars, *Bhandivadar, Mativadar* (Mannu Voddas), *Kalvadar (*Kallu Voddas) and *Gantadivadar* constituted four sub-divisions. The Bhandi-Vadars quarried and cut stones, dug tanks and sank wells. The Mati Vadars also did the masonry work. Inter-marriage and inter-dining were permissible between these two sub-castes. The Kal-Vadars quarried the stones and made grinding stones etc. Theirs was an endogamous group. Inter-marriages and interdining with others were forbidden. The Gantadi-Vadars' hereditary occupation was to build houses in the village. Some of them accepted the occupation of the rayats cultivating the *jirayat* lands and paying the *mohtarfa*. Their another occupation was to enter in disguise the crowds of the people at market places or fairs and to rob the people of their ornaments. This robbery was done during day only. Stealing at night was not permitted. If anybody stole at night, he was excommunicated. The *teravu* for the marriage was Rs. 150/- and that for the widow remarriage Rs. 300/-.

The *Kumbhars* forming another caste were found among the Lingayats, Velags, Banajewars and even Shudras. The *Bile Jadars* constituted the next caste which was also known as the *Patasili* caste. They worshipped Khaleshwar. They tied the Lingas round their necks. Hence their conduct was governed by the Lingayat rules. It was an endogamous group. The *Silavani Sonars* also had accepted Lingayatism. No details are found in the sources about the Kumbhar and Silavant Sonar Castes.

The priest of the *Uppars* was Kanakagirikar Shrivaishnava Acharya and the tutelary deities were Venkoba, Kanakagiri Kanakavirayya, Narasimha Swami, Hanamantadev, Hulagevva and Yellavva. They were not supposed to take country liquor (*sindi*) and wine (*sharab*). Their hereditairy occupations were to prepare salt pans, to build houses, to do agriculture and other similar jobs. In this caste there were three sub-castes called the 7-*hon* (*yelhon*) Uppars, 5-*Varahi* (*Aidvarai*) Uppars, and 8-*hon* Uppars. Inter-marriages and inter-dining between the 7-*hon* and 5-varahi Uppars were allowed, and not with the 8-*hon* Uppars. The division of house property, the custom of purification and excommunication, and also the celebration of festivals were governed by the rules of Telang Banajewars.

The *Hanagiwale Tatagars* were Muslims by religion but Hindu by caste and their occupation was to make the *banagis*. A sub-caste of the Marathas was called *Dadal*. They were the devotees of Hanuman and other Hindu gods. They had no priest. Some caste-man acted as the priest. Marriages and re-marriages were allowed. They did not take their meals with the members of any other castes except with the Lingayats. Spinning or knitting wool was their occupation. The rest of their conduct was like that of the Shudras. Division of property and the celebration of festivals were done as per the custom of the land. The *Dombars* were either Muslims or Marathas, but constituted a Hindu caste.

The members of the *Chhetri* caste were also known as Chitragars and Jinagars. Their priest was Shankar Bharati Swami. The usual Samskars they underwent. There was no remarriage. The Brahmins acted as Grampurohits. They put on the sacred thread, and no Linga. Inter-dining with the Brahmins only was allowed, not with other castes. They were non-vegetarians, but did not touch wine. They cremated their dead. Other practices were similar to those of other people in the land.

The *Nilagars, Shimpis* and *Rangare* were the next aritsan castes. Nilagars were dyers, specially indigo-dyers. The Shimpis were tailors, while the Rangares were painters. Their family god was Vithoba and goddess Tulajabhavani, the priest was their own caste-man. *Shendi, Lagna*, and *Shobhana* were performed by them. The girls married before puberty. Widow marriage was allowed. The *teravu* was 10 *hons* both for the marriage and the remarriage. They had neither the sacred thread nor the Linga on their bodies. They cremated their dead. They had 10 days of impurity or *sutaka* after the death of some one, on the 11th day they concluded this period with a sweet dish and performed *paksha* in the *Paksha* month. The Brahmins officiated at such rituals. They dined with Muslims and the members of other castes. They celebrated the Hindu festivals, and the division of property was done as per the custom of the land.

The *Dhobis* had a Hindu god and one of their caste-men was their priest. The properly was equally divided amongst the wives, and the property of each wife was again equally divided amongst her sons. Their occupation was to wash clothes.

The *Koraves* or *Koravis*[1] worshipped Venkataramana and Hanuman. They had no regular priest, but four of their caste-men acted as priests. There was no fixed marriageable age for boys and girls. Widow marriage was prevalent. They cremated their dead, if they were Namadharis, otherwise they were buried.

The division of property, like that of Dhobis, was done amongst the wives. The Hindu festivals were celebrated. Their occupation was to play the pipe (*vajantri*), to make (rough) grooms etc., and also brushes called *Koravi Kunchi*. Their occupation included, strangely enough, committing thefts at night. The things stolen were later properly divided among the persons concerned. The man who took the initiative and brought the things/valuables was given a bigger share and all others who helped him got equal shares from the remaining booty. They lived in huts. Besides theft, they also subsisted by agriculture. They did not commit theft during day. The member of the caste accepted his grand-daughter (daughter's daughter) as his daughter-in-law. If this daughter-in-law gave birth to a female baby, then this girl was given in marriage to her uncle's son. In other words both the uncle-niece marriage and the cross-cousin marriage were prevalent.

The *Sendiwale* constituted the next caste. Lord Nataraj was their tutelary god and the *ishta-deva* was Venkoba. Among their caste-men Katimaniwale Badamikar was the priest for this area, and Bankapurkar was for the Savanur area.

The Samskars were mainly three in number, *jawal, shendi* and *lagna*. The rules regarding these and other details were as usual. Their occupation was the sale of wine, etc. agriculture, if they had lands, and trade. The Brahmins officiated at their marriages.

The next caste was that of the *Kahars*. They were also known as *Gangimakal* caste people. Their god and goddesses were Mailarlinga,

1. According to Wilson, this is the name of a low tribe in Mysore, of which there are three branches — *Kala-Koravar*, who are professed thieves; *Walaga-Koravar*, who are musicians; and *Hakki-Koravar*, who are a migratory race, and subsist by making baskets, catching birds, etc. They are hill and forest tribes, and have a dialect of their own. (*Glossary*, p. 294).

Yellavva, Mahisasura-Mardini, Hulagi Hosur and Honakari Dev. Some one from their caste acted as the priest. *Javal, shendi, lagna, udaki, shobana* and the funeral rituals were performed as usual. In the division of property, the sons got equal shares. The festivals were celebrated as per the custom of the land. In addition they celebrated the *moharram* of the Muslims. Widow remarriage was allowed as the term *udaki* indicates.

If any body from the caste eloped with a member of another caste, or if he or she took wine or dined with a Muslim or a Berad, he or she was excommunicated from the caste, but could be taken back into the caste after purification. Their occupation was to serve as soldiers, to work as lime-burners or lime workers or as boatmen, to make sackbags or to weave cloth, to serve as carriers of torches and of palanquins. But they did not carry double water-skins called *pakhals*.

The *Bhois* were palanquin-bearers, the *Buruds* were basket-makers and the *Kalals* were distillers or vendors of spiritous liquor. The family god of the Bhois was Vyenkoba, and the priest was Shrivaishnava Acharya. They also worshipped Dariyadev, Khanderao and Yellamma. The Bhois had to pay 6 *hons* as the bride-price (*teravu*) for marriage and 10 rupees for remarriage. Carrying the palanquin, holding the umbrella and *abdagiri*, service and fishing were their hereditary occupations.

Godya Kahars seem to have constituted a sub-caste of this group. Their god was Kaledev of Hindusthan, and the priests were Kalimar and Nayojibava. The Samskars were like those of lower castes. However, the marriage dues (bride-price) were not taken here. Eating fowl or taking country liquor was forbidden. Adultery was heavily punished by excommunicating the culprits, who were or were not taken back into the community depending on the will of the community. Their occupation was carrying the palanquins, catching fish, agriculture, knitting, service etc.

Balabanis (also called Lamanis) or *Bajyas* were probably the natives of Jodhpur and Jaipur. Their family god and goddess were Vyenkoba and Bhavani and the priest was Gosavi. If a male child was born, the goats were distributed among the caste-people on the 5th and 7th days. There was no fixed marriageable age among these people. The marriage expenses were about 200 rupees besides the marriage *teravu* of 55 to 65 hons. Remarriage usually did not take place. They dined with Brahmins, Lingayats, Dhanagars and Uppars, and not with Muslims, Hajams Dheds, Berads, Karaves, and the like. If the latter rule was violated, the punishment would be excommunication. The women of this caste did not take non-vegetarian food, betel leaves and betelnuts, nor did they drink water from rivers and streams, where the water was flowing. But they took water from wells, lakes, tanks etc. As the male members were usually outside on the countryside going from place to place, they were allowed to take any water, and also local liquor and wine, betel leaves and betelnuts They could enjoy smoking from a *hooka*. They could also eat pork, but not at home.

In this caste the Rajput Brahmins, Marathas, Dheds, and Hajams (barbers) were also found. With the Rajputs, the remaining three could take meals, but not *vice versa*. With the Marathas the Hajams and Dheds took meals, but not *vice versa*. There were no inter-marriages among them.

The Rajputs had four surnames, namely, Rajput, Pawar, Jadhav and Ajad. The occupation of the Balabani caste was to trade in salt, foodgrains, wood etc., to make and sell sackbags and *sutali* (jute string). The women in this caste used to put on the bangles made of ivory and glass, and wore clothes decorated with shells. They had no ornaments of gold or silver. They used the sleeved breastcoat (*choli*) with the front side at the back, and the backside at the front.

The *Maheshwari* caste people worshipped the Hindu gods and goddesses such as Tulja Bhavani, Venkataramana, Virabhadra, Yellavva, Ishwar, Maruti, etc. and their priest was a Gosavi called Keshavapuri Bava Bijapur. The usual Samskars were undergone. Non-vegetarian food and wine were not taken. They could eat in the houses of Brahmins, Kshatriyas, Vaishyas and Lingayats. If they dined in the houses of other caste people except in the above ones, they were declared outcaste. If the Marathas cooked food in the house of the Maheshwari, then he could take it, but not in the house of the Maratha. The Mahashwaris did not even take water from the Shudra caste people. They did not put on the *Linga*, sacred thread etc., nor did they have sacred ashes nor the sacred *Nama*. But they applied sandal paste (*gandha*) and holy turmeric powder (*bhandara*). They had to take meals only after their bath. No remarriage was allowed. No bride-price was to be paid. Cross-niece marriages were prevalent. The girl was not married into outside families. The Brahmins officiated at marriages and other ceremonies. The festivals were celebrated as per the custom of the land.

The division of the property was usually done among the sons, unless there were some agreements to the contrary. Some of them put on the sacred thread, mudra, sandal paste called *gopi-chandan* and applied sacred ashes to their bodies. Their occupation was to prepare perfumes and to sell them. Besides, they were also general traders in their own land.

The *Hanamars* had Maruti as their family god, and no regular priest. However, the Katimaniwale would prescribe punishment for them in cases of commission of any undesirable deeds.

On the 5th day after the birth of a child they performed a ceremony called *iral*. On the 9th day the mother was taken to a river or to any other place where water was available naturally, the *Ganga-Pujan* was performed and a pot filled with water was brought home. That day the caste-women were fed. On the 12th the *jawal* ceremony was performed and in the third year the *shendi* was left. In the 12th year the marriage was performed. The girl had to marry preferably before puberty. She could remarry only once. The boy could marry as many times as he liked. The bride-price was paid at the rate of 5 *hons* for the marriage and 10 rupees for the remarriage. The tradition was that if the boy paid the *teravu*, then it was the responsibility of the girl's parent to bear all the expenses of celebrating the marriage. Widow remarriage was allowed.

The boy's marriage/remarriage was not performed in the village at home, but at the fold for kine or cowpen or the place where the cattle were huddled together or confined in the forest. The bride and the bridegroom were supposed to put on only white dress, and not the dress of any other colour. Again they were not supposed to wear the wedding head-gear called *basinga*. The caste people or the relatives had to stay in the forest itself and eat there only on the three days of the marriage ceremony. The *Shobhana* Samaskar was not performed, this practice was absent in this caste. They buried their dead, and observed 10 days' period of impurity, and then fed their caste people.

They did not dine with Muslims, Bedars, Koravis, Atishudras, and other lower caste people. They took animal flesh and wine. They ate the flesh of big animals such as buffaloes, cows, bullocks, and also of goats, fowl, etc. If someone violated the tradition of this caste, he was excommunicated. Later if the Katimaniwale and the caste-people so desired, such outcastes could be taken back into the caste after some purificatory rites. But those who committed whoredom were never taken back into the caste. The festivals observed were as per the custom of the land. The division of property was among the wives. Each of them would later equally divide the shares among their children. The occupation of the caste-people was to tend cattle, to build the folds for the kine, agriculture and service.

The *Yakar* caste had as their family deities Venkoba, Maruti, Yellavva, etc. and the priest was Kanakagirikar Shrivaishnava Acharya. Their Samskaras were more or less like those of other lower castes. They took mutton and fowl yearly once or so. Otherwise they did not touch them. Country liquor and wine they never took. They did not dine with Muslims, Bedars and Lohars. If somebody did dine violating this rule, he would be excommunicated. Interdining with the members of other castes was allowed. They did not put on either the *linga* or the *janawa*. But they were Namadharis, for they had got the *Name* or *symbol* impressed on their bodies. Elopement with the members of other castes led to their excommunication. If excommunicated for minor offences, they could be taken back into the caste after purification at the hands of Melagiri Naik.

The *Khowars* or *Telangi Brahmins* were superior to the three castes of Uppars, Telang Banajars and Bedars. The Khowars were called Kattimaniwale, and had the right to give the mudra-initiation etc. to the above three castes. The *Khowars* worshipped Vyenkoba and Kanakagirikar Narasimhaswami, and their priest was Kanakagirikar Shrivaishnava Acharya. They had the Samaskars of *jawal, shendi* and *lagna* following the usual rules and customs. They had the permission to dine with the Brahmins, Komatis, Lingayats, Redars, and Telang Banajewars. They did not have *janawa* or *linga* on their bodies. On the other hand they got the *Name* impressed on their body. The Brahmins officiated at their marriages.

The *Helawars* were the devotees of Hanamanta, Yellavva, Basappa, Ishwar, Venkoba, etc. They had no priest. A few members of their own caste people sat in judgement over them in cases of lapses in duties or violations of rules and gave initiation to the other members. They dined in the houses of all except in those of Dheds, Chamars and Salagars. The Dheds, Chamars etc. ate with the *Helawars*. They ate the flesh of crocodiles, big animals like the bullocks, and also fowl, goats, fish, deer, hares, etc. The division of property was made among the sons and also Basavis or spinsters supposed to have been dedicated to the god.

If anybody ate the flesh of the pig and committed adultery with a woman of the Dhed caste, he was excommunicated. If he offered country liquor and wine to his caste people, he was purified and taken back into the caste. If a woman eloped with a Dhed, then both man and woman were certainly not taken back into the caste. They cremated their dead, if they were Namadharis and Basavis, others were buried. They begged from Jamidars' houses and from their own caste people. Their occupation, in addition, was to prepare and sell country liquor, serve in various places, etc.

The *Atishudras* included such castes as Ramosi, Berad, or Bedar and the like. The *Bedars* worshipped Venkoba, Maruti, Yellavva etc., and their priests were Kanakagirikar Shrivaishnava Acharya and Kattimaniwale caste people. The *jawal* was done within three months after the birth of the child. The Dhanagar cut some hair of the child's head with the scissors with which he generally cut the hair of the goats, and the rest of the hair was cut by the barber. The ceremony of leaving the *shendi* or the tuft of hair was performed in a year. The girl had to marry before puberty. Remarriage also was allowed. There were Namadharis in this caste. If a female child was born she was not married, but left as a Basavi. This shows how low was the position of women in this caste.

These people ate the flesh of the bulls, cows and buffaloes. Only some people desisted from eating the flesh of these animals. They took wine and flesh in general. If any body committed whoredom or any other bad offence, he was excommunicated. They were later taken back into the caste after purification, only if the Kattimaniwale and caste people wished so.

The *Bedars* dined with the members of all castes, except with the Vadars, Koravis, Dasars, and Mahars. The division of the property was done equally among the wives.

In this caste there were two sub-divisions called *Gavache Bedar* and *Mayyache Bedar*. The latter Bedars underwent the ritual of *Sunati*, and until it was healed they lived in the forest only. This practice seems to have been similar to the practice of the Bedars of Bellary, Mysore, Chilradurga, Harapanahalli, etc. beyond the Tungabhadra.

These Bedars did not take country liquor and wine and also fowl. But they ate the flesh of bulls, buffaloes etc. As the Bedars ate the flesh of big animals, they were counted amongst Atishudras. But among the Atishudras they were superior.

The next caste was that of the *Mahars*, also called *Dheds*, and in Kannad *Holers*. Their tutelary goddess was Durgmurigewa and the priest was Sangoji Mangoji connected somehow with Pandharpur. *Jawal*, *shendi* and *lagna* were performed. Ramarriage was allowed. The *teravu* for the marriage was 5 *hons* and for the remarriage 2.50 *hons*. Among the dead, they cremated the Namadharis and buried the rest. The period of impurity was of 10 days, and on the 11th day the caste people were fed. They had the custom of illuminating the *mal* every year.

This was the custom of illuminating a garland of lamps before their family god once a year. Members of some castes felt that it was obligatory for them to burn the lamps before their god every year.

They ate the dead horses, donkeys and other big animals. They did not dine with the Mangs, but dined with the Dhors and Bedars. The girls were dedicated to the god as Basavis. Thereafter they never married. The division of the property was done among the wives. And the property of each wife was equally divided among her sons and Basavis. But the married girl did not get her share.

The Mahars did not do leather work. Their occupation was sweeping or cleaning, bringing wood, providing grass and leaves, etc. for the horses, camels, elephants and the like.

In the villages having Mangs these people had to do serfdom (*vetbigari*). The Mahar caste was superior to the Mang caste.

The *Mang* caste had as its tutelary goddesses Matangi and Yellavva, and its priest was Kanakagirikar Urava Koraya. *Javal*, *shendi* and *lagna* were the three important Samskars generally in all the lower castes, and this caste was no exception. The *teravu* here was 3.50 *hons* for the marriage and 2.25 *hons* for the widow remarriage. If dead, the *Namadharis* were cremated, and the rest were buried. The *sutak* or the period of impurity was generally of 10 days. On the 11th day the caste people were fed. There was no *mal*.

The dead camels, bulls, horses, cows, buffaloes, goats etc. were brought, cut, the share of the Mahars was given to them, and the rest was eaten by the Mangs. The elephant, donkey, dog and cat were not eaten, but the rest were eaten by the Mangs. These people did not dine with the cobblers, Samagars, Jinagars, Lingayats, barbers, etc., but dined with others. Even among the Mangs those who violated the rules or customs of the caste were excommunicated, and such outcastes lived outside the village, and they were called *Bemangs* among Mangs; the Mangs did not touch them, nor did they allow them to come to their places. However, they gave these outcastes food to eat. This food was eaten only by the outcastes, and not by others.

A sub-caste of this caste, called *Salagar* or *Samagar* caste also existed. The Salagars used to sit in the markets and make new sandals, besides repairing the old ones. In this caste the girls were converted into Basavis. The *Dhakalwales* were even inferior to the Samagars.

The *Chambhars* were the worshippers of Honakari Basaveshwar and their priest was known as Ganacharya. The Samskaras of *jawal, shendi* and *lagna* were undergone. Widow remarriage was allowed. The *teravu* was 5 *hons* for the marriage and 4 hons for the remarriage. They cremated their dead. After the period of impurity the caste people were fed on the 11th day after purification. The custom of *mal* they did not have. They did not eat pork, animals such as bulls, nor did they dine in the houses of those who ate such animals. The violation of this rule led to excommunication. If the wife eloped with a Dhed, she was excommunicated.

They took the flesh of fowl, goats, country liquor, and wine. They were superior to the Mahars and Mangs. Usually the Mahars and Mangs dined with the Chambhars except in some cases. On the other hand, the Chambhars did not dine with the Mahars and Mangs, and also with Dhors, Samagars, etc. Festivals and division of property were as per the custom of the land. Their occupation was to prepare new footwear and sell them off. The old ones were not repaired. If done so, the culprit was excommunicated. The leather was brought from the Dhors and Kasais. That was dyed and sold to these people by a sub-caste whose members were called *Samataniwale*.

The *Pakhal*-makers seem to have constituted a separate caste. They were said to have been descended from a certain Kakkayya. They prepared the double water-skin called 'pakhal'. Their tutelary god and goddess were Basaveshwar and Bhawani and the priest was Ganacharya. *Jawal, shendi, lagna* and udaki were performed. The practice of paying the *teravu* was not there. The period of impurity was of 12 days. Thereafter the caste people were fed. The *mal* was done once in a year. They did not eat the flesh of buffaloes, bulls and pigs, nor did they dine in the houses of Mahars and Mangs who ate these animals, and also with the Jain Muslims, Bedars, Vadars, Kors, Mochis, etc.

Their occupation was bringing leather from the Mangs, and selling it after making it usable, and also the preparation with that leather the double water-skin (*pakhal*), the small leather-bag carried under the arms (*masak*), the leather bucket to draw water from the draw-well (*mot*), round leather bags (*tokari*) etc. Festivals were celebrated as per the custom of the land. The division of property was among the wives. They took wine and flesh. The rules regarding excommunication, and also taking the excommunicated members back into the caste in minor cases were observed.

Finally, the Samagars, although forming a part of the Mang caste, were still different from the latter in some cases. Interdining and inter-marriage between the two were not allowed. They were two endogamous groups. Their occupation was to prepare sandals with the leather purchased and to sell them, and also to repair the old sandals sitting in the market.

Thus the rules and regulations governing the various castes and communities in the Southern Maratha Country during the Maratha period were very rigid. There were a number of endogamous groups constituting castes and sub-castes, and the members were very strict about dining practices and marriage customs, among other things. If these rules were violated, usually the culprits were excommunicated or punished in some other ways. For officiating at marriage ceremonies and other functions each caste had, as a rule, its own priest. Similarly each caste had its own tutelary deity or deities. The caste members had to worship these deities, because this practice was handed down to them from generation to generation. As it was a very rigid society bound down to various customs and practices by a multiplicity of rules, it was very difficult, nay, impossible, for any member of the caste, to give up such practices and strike out new paths for himself.

Among the Brahmins, the Shaivas evidently worshipped Lord Shiva or some other Shaiva gods as their tutelary deities. Similarly the Vaishnavas had Lord Vishnu, or one of his incarnations or some other Vaishnava gods as their family deities. It was not only the male gods but also their consorts that were apparently worshipped in these families. Besides these family deities, whose number could be large in some cases, each had the freedom to have his or her own favourite god or goddess (*ishta-devata*) and this would be a personal deity, not a caste or family deity.

Some examples, given already in a different context, may be noted here. The Vaishyas or Komatis had as their tutelary deities Nageshwar and Bhavani, the Padmasalis Venkoba and Lakshmi, and the Banagars Virabhadra. The Gollars, the Telang Banajewars, and the Mushtigers worshipped Venkoba only as their family god. Lord Venkoba or Vyenkatesha or Venkataramana, generally with His Consort Lakshmi, was the family deity of a number of caste-people. In some cases Venkoba along with Hanamanta Dev became the tutelary deity. Thus the Vadars or Voddas, and the Koraves or Koravis worshipped both Venkoba and Hanumanta. In some castes a number of deities were worshipped. For example, the Maheshwaris were the worshippers of Venkataramana, Tulaja Bhawani, Virabhadra, Yellavva, Ishwar, Maruti etc. Some of the lower classes worshipped, in addition to some of the above deities, evil spirits personified as some gods and goddesses, and also some local deities. Such deities were, for example, Birappa, Honakari Dev etc. The local gods were usually raised to a higher level by adding the suffix Ishwara to them, as in the case of Khaleshwar.

Among the gurus or priests that these castes had, most of the lower castes had a Shrivaishnava Acharya living at Kanakagiri which is now in the Raichur district of Karnataka. It appears that these lower folk came under the influence of Shrivaishnavism of Ramnujacharya who was at Melkote during the later period of his life. And Karakagiri also seems to have become an important Shrivaishnava centre in Karnataka. The Shrivaishnava Acharya at this place, therefore, was accepted as the priest of many castes in the Southern Maratha Country. Next, an orthodox family called Kattimani in most of the village assumed the role of the priest to many castes in this area. To some higher castes Shankara Bharati or the pontiff of the Shringeri Math occupied the position of the priest. To some others a Gosavi, the head of a religious institution, and usually a mendicant, became the priest. And in those families who had no regular priests, some of their own caste people who were influential, orthodox, and respected, acted as the priests. These priests generally officiated at various ceremonies in the caste and also sat in judgement over the people whenever they violated some caste rules. Such was the rigid control exercised over the caste members by these priests.

Among the tutelary deities worshipped by these castes Venkoba and some goddesses took the first rank, and next to them were Maruti and Ishwar. If the statistics about these details for the leading 46 castes are worked out, we find that 15 castes worshipped Venkoba as their tutelary god, and 2 castes as their favourite deity or *ishta-devata*, while 17 castes worshipped the goddess in some form or the other. Two castes worshipped Her as Tulaja Bhawani, 3 as Bhawani, 9 as Yellavva or Yellamma, 1 each as Lakshmi, Sirasangi Kalavva, Hulagevva, Mahishasura Mardini, Durgmurigevva, Matangi and Bana-Shankari. Maruti was worshipped as Hanuman or Hanumanta also. Similarly Ishwar was also worshipped as Nageshwar, Mahadev, Mailar Linga, Nataraj, and Khaleshwar. The other deities worshipped included Virabhadra, Birappa, Khandoba, Honakarideva, Kanakavirayya, Narasimha Swami, Vithoba, Dariyadeva, Kaledeva, Basappa and Basaveshwar.

Thus do we see that among the goddesses Yellavva or Yellamma was very popular. The word means 'Mother of all' So these were the worshippers of Mother Goddess. Kalavva was again a Mother Goddess coming from a village called Sirasangi Durgmuragi was a local deity propitiated for warding off evil spirits and pestilences. Hulagevva and Matangi were also the local deities finally, except Lakshmi who was the Consort of Lord Vishnu, all the rest were different forms of Parvati, the Consort of Lord Shiva. Among other gods Virabhadra, Khandoba Vithoba and Narasimha are well known. Here the last one is particularly the god coming from Kanakagiri. Birappa and Basappa were the gods of agriculturists, while Honakarideva also seems to be Basappa of the Honakari village as suggested by the term Honakari Basaveshwar and in one case of Hulagi Hosur also. Dariyadeva must have been a sea-god and Kaledeva or Kalledeva indicates animistic practices.

Among the priests Shrivaishnava Acharya was very popular, since he ranks first. He was the priest of 10 castes, while the jangam was the priest of 3 castes, the Kattimaniwale of 3, the Brahmin of 1, Shankara Bharati Swami of 1, Ganacharya of 2, the Gosavi of 2, and finally the caste-men or some local holy men were the priests of others. If we take the Jangam and Ganacharya together, then Lingayat priests were very popular next to the Shrivaishnava priest. The holy men that were accepted as priests by one or two castes in the society were Dharmada Ayya, Bankapurkar, Kalimar, Nayojibava, Keshavapuri Bawa Bijapur who was a Gosavi, Sangoji Mangoji, Urava Koraya of Kanakagiri and Devagayya of Hampi Math. Only one caste (Komatis) accepted a Brahmin as its priest. Although the Brahmin was generally not a priest of the castes, he was in most cases invited to officiate at the marriage and other ceremonies. Although the above deities were tutelary deities mentioned in the *Kaifiyats*, we find many others in other contemporary and earlier Modi documents. For example, a Zada of Varshasanas to temples and religious grants to Brahmins, etc in Pargana Kundagol[1] dated 1767 mentions a number of gods and goddesses to whom the temples were dedicated. Some of them have already been mentioned in the *Kaifiyats*, the remaining ones include Someshwar, Durgadevi, Gramadevati, Harihareshwar, Ganapati, Mallikarjun, Bhuteshadeva, Gangadhareshwar, Ramachandradeva and Ramalinga. Basavanna and Hanamanta of various localities are often mentioned. Gramadevati is a village goddess found universally in some name or the other. Ganapati is a new name here, the other names being some form of Lord Shiva or Vishnu. We have similar other documents where also we find various names of Lord Shiva or Vishnu.

I have already indicated earlier that the Brahmin and Maratha caste members held high posts in the administration. Only sometimes the Lingayats were favoured. The reason is that only some Lingayats were high caste Lingayats, otherwise a large number of them belonged to the lower castes. Lingayatism was basically a faith, and not a caste. Those belonging to the lower castes accepted Lingayatism for improving their social status and for getting rid of social disabilities. Such converts naturally did not get high posts in the administration. They had to be satisfied with being the members of their own castes, but with a different faith. In respect of occupation they remained where they were, but in respect of social status their position was raised because of their new faith. We find a large number of such people in various documents belonging to different years. For example, a revenue document called *Sist Peth*

1. KJ: 77 : 339.

Haveri[1] of Khamas Tisain Maya va Alaf (1795 A.D.), Mahe Rabilawal, gives us a list of merchants in the market of Haveri from whom the tax was collected. These include members belonging to various castes, some of whom had accepted Lingayatism. Gurasiddavva Teli (a member of the Ganiger caste), Totya Ainapur (a Lingayat), Masur Madivalappa (a low-caste man), Tukaji Bhogar (another low-caste man), Suganna Sonar (a goldsmith), Mulgund Sivabasanna (a Lingayat), Anapya Jainar (a Jain), Simpi (a tailor), Uppar Fakiranna (a salt-maker by caste), Mahalingappa (a Lingayat), Ija Nalabandi (a cobbler), Kasai (a member of the Kasai caste), and the like. In 1767 A.D. the *Muzarian* of Qasba Dharwad[2] included Basanna Ainapur (a Lingayat), Imam Ladkhan (a Muslim), Denanna Durmuri (a Mahar or Holeya), Tipur Setti (a Vaishya or Komati), Kurabar Bharamanna (a shepherd), Sultanji Marathe (a Maratha by caste), Kumbhars, Koshtis, Bagadibars, Jalagar Momins (Muhammadan weavers), Khatibs, Qazis, etc.

In the northern part of Southern Maratha Country the caste-members included Kadapa Bhusar (a grain-dealer), Guravayya Jangam (a Lingayat priest), Daraji Yani (a tailor),[3] Lavhar Sutar (a carpenter)[4], Sadashiv Wani (a member of the Wani caste, a retail dealer), Chennappa Dhanagar (a shepherd by caste), Basha Nahavi (a barber), Nimbaji Parit (a washerman), Bhujanga Chambhar (a cobbler), Lakshya Mang (a member of the Mang caste)[5], and the like.

There were a number of Muslims in the Southern Maratha Country. Although there were very few earlier, yet during the rule of the Bahamani Sultans, Bijapur Adilshahs and Savanur Nawabs, their number gradually increased. As is well known, Allah was their God. There were 14 Pirs such as Hajrat Imam Hussein, his disciple Rayan Khan and their predecessors, and the decendants of these Pirs were the priests of the Muslims in this area. Soon after the birth of the child, '*Anja*' was recited, and the child was made to drink milk. On the 40th day the naming ceremony was performed. Next the Bismilla ceremony was performed at the appropriate time. Then from the 5th to the 7th year the *Sunata* was done, and the poor were fed. The boy was to marry between the 16th and 20th year of his age, while the girl was to marry 6 months before puberty. Man could have a maximum of 4 wives at a time, and after the death of the husband the widow could remarry, if she so desired. They buried their dead.

1. KJ: 177 : 348.
2. KJ: 51 : 147.
3. KJ: 177 : 351.
4. KJ: 177 : 352.
5. KJ: 1072 : 335.

They celebrated the following festivals every year:

Month	**Festival details**
Muharram	10 days'-festival
Safar	2 festivals
Rabilawal	12th day-*Urus*
Rabilakhar	11th day, one-day festival in the name of the Pir.
Jamadilawal	16th day-*Urus*
Jamadilakhar	11th day, one-day festival in the name of Fateh Pir.
Rajjab	Festival in the name of Masud Qazi on every Thursday.
Shaban	14th day, Fatah in the name of the Pir.
Ramzan	Fast for 30 days, and meals at night.
Shavval	Fatah in the name of Gabar. All the Muslims to go out of the village, do *Namaz* and hear the *Khutba*.
Jilkad	16th day, Festival in the name of Khwaja Banda Nawaz
Jilhej	10th day, Fatah to be done in the name of Ismail Paigambar; All the Muslims to do *Namaz* and hear the *Khutba*.

Besides these, the minor festivals were to be celebrated as per the custom of the land.

The division of property was to be done equally between sons and daughters. However, this rule was not strictly followed by the Muslims. The cross-cousin marriage was allowed. The Muslims here were of four types, Shaikh, Sayyid, Mughal, and Pathan, and these were exogamous groups.[1]

During the Adilshahi rule, there were naturally a large number of Muslims manning both major and minor posts in the administration. In the administrative machinery at the Subha, Paragana and Tarf levels there were usually Muslim officials. However, at the village level there were the hereditary Hindu officials. When we come to the Maratha period the Muslim officials were gradually replaced by the Hindu officials, mostly the Brahmin and Maratha officials. At the village level

1. *Sannika* : 54.

there were usually Lingayats. However, among the Barabalute or village servants there were persons coming from different castes and also the Muslims. Like the Mahars, the Muslims also had great importance in the local administrative set-up. Besides, some of them were in charge of mosques or acted as priests for the Muslim population. Sometimes these got lands in *inam* or *mukasa* or *dumala* from the rulers. All this is borne out by the contemporary reliable administrative documents.

In 1658 A.D. Sidi Yusuf Poladkhan was an officer over the Desai and Deshkulkarni of Pargana Rayara Hubli.[1] In 1669 Sherif Mahmad Khan was over the Deshmukhs, Deshpandes, and Mukaddams of Pargana Rayara Hubli.[2] Muslims were found as Inamdars or holders of *dumalegaons*, as archers and rocket-bearers. In 1793 Abu Miya Hadin and two Muslim Fakirs were the holders of *dumalegaons* in Pargana Adur. Two *dumalegaons* were enjoyed by Syed Nasir-ud-din-Pirjade in Pargana Hangal.[3] In 1794 Shaikh Manula, Shaikh Hussein, Inayet Khan and Alal were archers or rocket-bearers while Allah Baksh and Amin Shah were Gardis in the Savanur Taluka of Southern Maratha Country. The Gardis worked under Sadashiv Krishna and Dhondo Balal Sathe. The Gardis that were trained better were under Ismail Khan.[4] Villages or part of the revenue were often granted to the Muslim religious institutions. In 1793 three villages were granted in Pargana Ranebennur to the Muslim religious institutions including the *darga* of Jamal Saheb, and Pirjade. Two villages in Pargana Nidsangi were also for Pirjade, one for Mahamad Saheb Pir, and the other for the tomb of the Savanurkar Nawab.[5]

Some other Muslims were found as Mulanas or village school masters, as Kazis or Muhammadan judges or law experts or in some other capacity. In a *Yadi* of Pargana Nave Hubli 3 *hons* were paid in 1764 to a Mulana.[6] In 1797 1 *mar* or 36 bighas of sarvamanya or inam lands were with the Kazi in the village of Yellapur.[7] Among the village officials of Rayera Hubli were Naik bin Husseini Naik, Hasan Naik bin Miya Naik and Kazi Mahmad. Among the Deshaks was Hasan Naik.[8] In the village these positions carried with them much prestige and honour. In Lakkundi of Pargana Gadag we find a number of Muslims either occupying positions

1. BISMA, Belagali Desai Daftar: 511.
2. BISMA, Belagli Desai Daftar: 510.
3. KJ: 246.
4. KJ: 245.
5. KJ: 246.
6. KJ: 66 : 712.
7. KJ: 63 : 870.
8. BISMA, Khare Daftar, S.No. 541, dated probably in 1753 A.D.

of importance in the administration or in possession of inam lands, or as Varatdars or as ordinary employees. Such were Adam Khan, Abdul Nabi, Mahmad Burhan, Sheikh Rasul, Sheikh Latif Fazl, Mahmad Sale Fazl, Sheikh Sultan, Sheikh Hussein, Sheikh imam, Miya Khan, Mirza Beg, Sheikh Usman, Sheikh Mohi-ud-din, Mavdan Khan, Bahadar Khan, and the like.[1] In the same Tarf in 1811 A.D. a Nadaf, a cotton clearner, was paying 1.50 *hons* as a tax[2] This was in the month of Jamadilwal, when Shrinivas Lakshman was its Kamavisdar. However in the month of Ramzan, Nadaf Gajabar was paying one *hon* as *mohtarfa*.[3] It is difficult to identify Nadaf with Nadaf Gajabar. In Pargana Azamnagar (modern Belgaum) in 1816 A.D. the Siwaye Jama included 10 rupees from Seriban Musalman, 35 from Khatija Maula, 21 from Habita Musalman, 5 from Khatija, and 10 from Syed Kadar. The *Sibandi* or local militia included Sheikh Imam, Hussein, Sheikh Ibrahim, Syed Gaffur and others.[4]

Thus was this society honey-combed with castes and sub-castes, with tribes and communities, with Muslims and their sub-divisions and with a sprinkling of Christians. There were differences between higher castes, and lower castes, among higher castes between Brahmins and non-Brahmins, among Brahmins between *Shatkarmis* and *Trikarmis*, and among them between *Trikarmis* and non-*Trikarmis*. Among the lower castes there were differences between Shudras and Atishudras and among Atishudras between Mahars and Mangs. Again within many castes there were endogamous groups having differences between them. Almost all the castes were desirous of performing the 16 Samskaras. As it was either not possible or not permitted to do so, at least the *jawal*, *shendi* and *lagna* were adhered to, and after death the funerary rites were strictly performed. The castes performing lesser Samskaras were looked down upon by those performing more Samskars or the so-called higher castes. Similarly the castes practising divorce and widow remarriage were despised by those who did not allow divorce and remarriage, and therefore who thought themselves purer than the former. The funerary rites insisted on observing a period of impurity following the death of a person, and were thereafter purified ritualistically. The endogamous groups invariably considered themselves purer than, and so superior to, the exogamous groups. The lower castes such as Mahars and Mangs, because of their position in the Barabalute system, had an important position in the economic set-up of the village, although in the social

1. KJ: 157 : 547.
2. KJ: 157 : 530.
3. KJ: 157 : 534.
4. KJ: 271 : 166.

hierarchy they were at the lowest rung. The violation of the caste rules led to excommunication, and the culprits might or might not be taken back into the caste depending upon the will of the people or caste elders.

The caste system seemed to be inexorable, and the various castes, sub-castes, tribes, classes and communities were inseparably fitted into this steel framework, people born in various castes being bound down to their own customs and practices, finding no way to come out of them, forced as they were to accept their lot as their destiny. In such a system man had no freedom of thought and action, his initiative was stiffled, his enterprise crushed, his enthusiasm pulled down, and his hopes dashed to the ground. Even the Brahmins who were at the apex of this system were divided among themselves, and although they were considered to be superior to others, were yet bound down to their own rites and rituals, to their own customs and manners, to their own miseries and weaknesses arising out of a deplorable lack of the spirit of social freedom and enterprise. Even in the religious field their minds were putrefied, having been compelled to accept many of the worthless religious ideas and conventions blindly handed down from generation to generation. Such a society gave rise to a large section of social serfs and intellectual slaves, to a small body of the privileged class enjoying its position at the cost of others, to the irrational ideas of untouchability and purity and to the despicable position of women. Thus the whole society was based on the principle of inequality and on the slavery of thought and action. It was enveloped in the darkness of meaningless customs and manners, although illumined from time to time by streaks of lightning of real wisdom and true spirituality.

CHART ON THE CASTES IN THE SOUTHERN MARATHA COUNTRY DURING THE MARATHA PERIOD

S.No.	Caste	Venkoba	Maruti	Ishwar	Other Gods	Goddess	Guru
1.	Brahmins						
	Vaishnavas	[Vishnu]					
	Shavas			[Shiva]			
2.	Kshatriyas						
3.	Vaishyas or Komatis				Nageshwar	Bhawani	Brahmin
4.	Jains				Mahavira		
5.	Shudras						
6.	Lingayats			Ishwar			
7.	Marathas						
8.	Redars	Venkoba					Shrivaishnava Acharya
9.	Padmasalis	Venkoba				Lakshmi	Shrivaishnava Acharya
10.	Banagars				Virabhadra		Jangam
11.	Gollas	Venkoba			Krishnadeva		Shrivaishnava Acharya
12.	Telang	Venkoba					Shrivaishnava Acharya
	Benajewars						
13.	Mushtigers	Venkoba					Shrivaishnava Acharya

S.No.	Caste	Venkoba	Maruti	Ishwar	Other Gods	Goddess	Guru
14.	Telis						
15.	Jirs or Garavis			Mahadev			Jangam
16.	Dhangars		Hanamappa	Mailara Linga	Birappa Khandoba Honakarideva	Yellamma	Caste-man
17.	Hande Kurabis						
18.	Panchals					Sirasangi Kalavva	Caste-man Dharmada Ayya
19.	Jalagars						
20.	Voddas	Venkoba	Hanamanta-deva				Shrivaishnava Acharya
21.	Kumbhars						
22.	Bile Jadars			Khaleshwar			
23.	Silavant Sonars						
24.	Uppars	Venkoba	Hanamanta-deva		Kanakavirayya	Hulagevva, Narasimha swami	Yellavva
25.	Hanagiwale Tatagars		Hanuman				Casteman

S.No.	Caste	Venkoba	Maruti	Ishwar	Other Gods	Goddess	Guru
26.	Dombars						Shankara Bharati Swami
27.	Chhetris or Chitragars or Jinagars						
28.	Nilagars Shimpis and Rangare				Vithoba	Tulja Bhavani	Caste-man
29.	Dhobis				Hindu god		Caste-man
30.	Koraves or Koravis	Venkataramana	Hanuman				Caste-man
31.	Sendiwale	Venkoba	Ashta-deva	Natraj		Bankapurkar	Katimaniwale
32.	Kahars			Mailara Linga	Hulagi Hosur Honakarideva	Yellavva Mahisasura Mardini	Caste-man
33.	Bhois Buruds kalals	Venkoba			Dariyadeva Khanderao	Yellamma	Shrivaishanava Acharya
34.	Godya Kahars				Kalidev	Kalimar	
35.	Balabanis or Bajyars	Venkoba				Bhavani	Nayajibava Gosavi
36.	Maheshwaris	Venkataramana	Maruti	Ishwar	Virabhadra	Tulja Bhavani Yellavva	Gosavi Called Keshavapuri

S.No.	Caste	Venkoba	Maruti	Ishwar	Other Gods	Goddess	Guru
							Bawa Bijapur
37.	Hanamars		Maruti				Nil/Katimaniwal
38.	Yakars	Venkoba	Maruti			Yellavva	Shrivaishnava Acharya
39.	Khowars or Telangi Brahmins	Venkoba			Narasimhaswami of Kanakagiri	Shrivaishnava Acharya	
40.	Helawars	Venkoba	Hanumanta	Ishwar	Basappa	Yellavva	Caste-men
41.	Bedars	Venkoba	Maruti			Yellavva	Shrivaishnava Acharya and Kattimaniwale
42.	Mahars or Dheds or Holers					Durgmurige	Sangoji Mangoji
43.	Mangs					Matanagi	Urava Koraya of Kanakagiri
						Yellavva	
44.	Chambars				Honkari Basaveshwar		Ganacharya
45.	Pakhal-makers				Basaveshwar	Bhawani	Ganacharya
46.	Koshtis or Hatagars						

Select Bibliography

Primary Sources

(*Unpublished*)

Pune Archives

Karnatak Jamav, Bundle Nos. 49, 51, 62, 77, 82, 95, 157, 158, 163, 177, 224, 226, 228, 239, 240, 241, 242, 243, 245, 246, 263, 270, 271, 274, 301, 323, 324, 325, 339, 349, 364, 373, 374, 375, 376, 387, 434, 453, 467, 531, 553, 554, 816, 822, 843, 1072, 1095, 1597, 1905, 1929, 1943.

Kaifiyats, Bundle No. 1597

Ghadni Bundle Nos. 640, 453

Deccan Commissioners' Files, Vol. No. 224

Papers selected for Research (Sannika) Bundle No. 1

Budhgaon Daftar

Bombay Archives

Vol. No. 162/A : A Diary of the Transactions of the Hon'ble Company's Affairs at Carwar by Robert Holford Revenue Department (RD) Vol. No. 97/1181 of the year 1840: Mohtarfa Taxes : Mr. Langford's Report on the Konkan and S.M. Country.

Bharat Itihas Samshodhak Mandal Archives

Belagali Desai Daftar

Dikshit-Patwardhan Daftar

G.H. Khare collection

Goshala Raste Daftar

Lakshmeshwar Desai Papers, Nos. LD. 25, 148, 150, 153, 160, 162, 163, 183, 184, 190, 191, 192, 256, 318, 340/B, 341/A, 387.

Malikwadkar Daftar, Bundle Nos. 5, 6, 7, 9, 10, 11, 12, 13-24, 27, 28.

Ramtirth Temple Papers, Nos. *PU* 27, 28, 39, 40, 53, 59, 96, 105, 106, 110.

Andhra State Archives

Hukmnama of Tipu Sultan

Partagali Math Archives

Inward Letter Book

Jamabandi Papers

Mortgage Deeds

Sale-deeds

Kolhapur Archives

Torgal Daftar

Deccan College Archives

Kittur Papers, Bundle No. 74, File No. 8.

Karnatak Archives

Box No. 9

Sheshadri Papers, Nos. 30, 138, 141, 158, 159, 218

Ramdurg Palace Daftar

Ajnapatra of Bijirao Raghunath

Nemnuk Beheda of Yogirao and Bhaskarrao

Dadaji of Nargund

Order of Sawayi Madhavrao to Lingoji

Gaikwad Hawaldar

Sanad of Govind Bhikaji Subhedar of Mamle

Torgal

Nargund Pujari Daftar: Over 400 papers

Grant of land to Srinivasbhat of Sirur

Sanad to Onkar Mahadev Kamavisdar, Inamat

Nargund.

Keladi Museum Archives

Inampatra to Mallappa Nadgir of Samat Tilavalli

Kaulnama to Lingappa

Deshkulkarni of Samat Tilavalli

Field Work

On the spot study of:

Dharwad fort
Ramdurg Fort
Savanur Fort
Gokak
Hirekerur
Nargund

PRIMARY SOURCES

(*Published*)

Aithihasika Lekha-Sangraha, ed. by V.V. Khare

Aitihasika Pharsi Sahitya

Aitihasika Sankima Sahitya: Sources of Medieval History of the Deccan, 3 vols. ed. by G.H. Khare, Pune, 1930-49.

Bombay Karnatak Inscriptions, Vol. IV, ed. by G.S. Gai, Delhi, 1965.

Basatin-us-salatin, of Muhammad Ibrahim Zubairi, Marathi translation by N.V. Parasnis, ed. by V.S. Bendrey, Bombay, 1968.

Inscriptions in Northern Karnataka and the Kolhapur State, ed. by K.G. Kundangar, Kolhapur, 1939.

Jijabai-Kalina-Kagadapatre, ed. by A.G. Pawar, Kolhapur, 1978.

Kaifiyals, Yadis etc. selected by G.C. Vad, Bombay, 1908.

Karavir Chhalrapatinchya Gharanyachi Kagadapatre, ed. by M.V. Gujar, 8 vols.

Karavir Riyasatichi Kagadapalre, ed. by S.M. Garge, Vol. 1, Pune, 1970, Vol. II, Pune, 1972, Vol. III, Pune, 1973, Vol. IV, Pune, 1982.

Karavir Sardaranchya Kaifiyati ed. by K.A. Gaikwad, Kolhapur, 1971.

Kitab Nawab Mustatabamo Allah Alakab Nawab Dalerkhan Bahadur Dalerjang Yanche Kharuiancha Ahwal, briefly called Dilerjangi, Dharwad, 1860 (Litho-print).

Muhammadnamah, extracts trarrs. into Marathi in the *Shiva-Charitra-vrittasangraha.*

Sabhasad, Krishnji Anant, Chhatrapati Shri Shivaji Raje Yanchi Bakhar (in Marathi), ed. by S.N. Joshi, Poona, 1960.

Savanur Nawabs: Historical Documents, ed. by K.N. Chitnis, Pune, 1985.

Selections from the Peshwa-Daftar Vol. Nos. 28, 31, 37, 39, 41, 43, ed. by G.S. Sardesai.

Selections from the Satara Raja's and Peshivas' Diaries, 9 vols., ed by G.C. Vad, Poona.

Shiva-Charitra Sahitya

Shiva-Kalina Patra-Sara-Sangraha, 3 vols.

Taha va Kararmadar, compiled and edited by G.C. Vad, pub. by D.B. Parasnis, Poona, 1914.

Shiva-Charitra-Pradip, ed. by D.V. Apte and N.C. Kelkar, Poona, 1925-
Jedhe Shakavali, published in the *Shiva-charitra-Pradip*.

Shivaji-Mallammaji Samarotsava, ed. by K.N. Chitnis, publisher: Kannada Department, University of Bombay, 1990.

Tarabai-Kalina Kagadapatre, ed. by A.G. Pawar, Kolhapur, Vol. I, 1969, Vol. II, 1970, Vol. III, 1972.

ADMINISTRATIVE REPORTS, MEMOIRS, MEMORANDA etc.

Chaplin, William, *Report exhibiting a view of the Fiscal and Judicial system of Administration introduced into the conquered Territory above the Ghats, Bombay*, 1824.

Kolhapur Ani Southern Maratha Country States che San 1921 isvi salachya khanesumariche Gaonvar va Dharmavar Lokasankhyeche Pustak, by Yeshwant Vinayak Ranadive, Kolhapur, 1922.

Selections from the Records of the Bombay Government, No. XII : *Reports on the Revenue Survey Settlements of the* Hoobullee, Nuwulgoond, Kode, and Dharwar Talookas of the Dharwar Collectorate, by Captain G. Wingate, Bombay, 1853.

Ibid., No. CLXI-New series : *Papers relating to the Revision of the Rates of Assessment* on the expiration of the first settlement in the old Dharwar Taluka of the Dharwar Collectorate, Bombay, 1883.

West, E.W, *A Memoir of the States of the Southern Maratha Country*, Bombay, 1869.

MODERN WORKS

Choksey, R.D., *Economic Life in the Bombay Karnatak* (1818-1939), Bombay, 1963.

Kamat, A.R., *Essays on Social Change in India*, Bombay, 1983.

Modak, B.P., *Kolhapur Va Kamatak Prantatil Rajye va sumsthan yancha Itihas* : Uttarardha, Bhag 2: *Karnataka Prantatil Samsthanancha Itihas, Belgaum,* 1880.

Modak, D.S. *The Bombay Land System and Village Administration*, Poona, 1932.

Saletore, B.A. and P.B. Desai, *Kannada Nadina Charitre* (in Kannada).

Satish Chandra, *Medieval India: Society, the Jagirdari Crisis and the Village*, Delhi, 1982.

Sherwani, H.K., and P.M. Joshi (ed), *History of Medieval Deccan (1295-1724)*, 2 vols. Hyderabad, 1973-74.

Sinha, N.K. *Haidar Ali*, Calcutta, 1949

Sinha, S.K., *Medieval History of the Deccan* 2 vols., Hyderabad, 1964, and 1968 respectively.

Varma D.C., *History of Bijapur*, New Delhi, 1974.

Wilson, H.H., *A Glossary of Judicial and Revenue Terms*, etc. 2nd ed., Delhi, 1968.

Wood, Captain (Compiler), History of Kolhapur, 1902, (in manuscript form)

JOURNALS AND PERIODICALS

Bharat Itihas Samshodhak Mandal Quarterlies, Pune.

Journal of Bombay Historical Society, Bombay.

Journal of Indian History, Trivandrum.

Karnatak Historical Review, Dharwad.

Quarterly Journal of Mythic Society, Bangalore.

Index

C

H

I

J

K